Psalm 23

THE SHEPHERD WITH ME

JENNIFER ROTHSCHILD

Lifeway Press® Nashville, Tennessee

Published by Lifeway Press® • © 2018 Jennifer Rothschild
Reprinted July 2021

No part of this book may be reproduced or transmitted in any form or by any means, electronic or mechanical, including photocopying and recording, or by any information storage or retrieval system, except as may be expressly permitted in writing by the publisher. Requests for permission should be addressed in writing to Lifeway Press®; One Lifeway Plaza; Nashville, TN 37234-0152.

ISBN: 978-1-4300-5498-6 • Item: 006103962

Dewey decimal classification: 223.2
Subject headings: BIBLE. O.T. PSALMS 23--STUDY AND TEACHING / WOMEN / SELF-CONFIDENCE

To order additional copies of this resource, write Lifeway Resources Customer Service; One Lifeway Plaza; Nashville, TN 37234; Fax order to 615.251.5933; call toll-free 800.458.2772; email orderentry@lifeway.com; or order online at www.lifeway.com.

Printed in the United States of America

Adult Ministry Publishing • Lifeway Resources • One Lifeway Plaza • Nashville, TN 37234

CONTENTS

ABOUT THE AUTHOR

Psalm 23: The Shepherd with Me is Jennifer's sixth video-based Bible study with Lifeway. It follows her popular Bible studies, *Hosea: Unfailing Love Changes Everything*; *Missing Pieces: Real Hope When Life Doesn't Make Sense*; and *Me, Myself, and Lies: A Thought-Closet Makeover*.

Jennifer became blind when she was fifteen years old and has experienced firsthand how God's companionship gives her comfort and confidence in every season of her life. Now more than thirty years later, as an author and speaker, she boldly and compassionately teaches women how to trust God in every season too.

Known for her substance, signature wit, and down-to-earth style, Jennifer weaves together relatable stories with biblical truths to help women know and live for Christ. She has shared her practical and inspiring messages to audiences across the country and through media outlets including *The Dr. Phil Show*, *Good Morning America*, *Life Today*, and *The Billy Graham Television Special*.

She is the featured teacher and founder of Fresh Grounded Faith Conferences and publisher of the popular online resource for women in ministry called womensministry.net.

Jennifer and her husband, whom she calls her "very own Dr. Phil," live in Missouri, and have two sons, Connor and Clayton, and a lovely daughter-in-law, Caroline. In 2017, she became a GiGi to her first grandbaby, and that's her favorite name of all!

Besides walking—or being walked by—her little dog, Lucy, Jennifer enjoys riding a bicycle built for two with her husband. She is also an avid listener of audio books, a C. S. Lewis junkie, and loves dark chocolate and robust coffee—especially when shared with a friend.

Connect with Jennifer at JenniferRothschild.com/Psalm23.

INTRODUCTION

Hey, girl! Thanks for spending the next few weeks with me walking through each verse of Psalm 23. You will be blown away by how much big truth is packed in this little psalm. I sure was. I still am.

Psalm 23 changed my whole understanding of God's love and care for me, and it's giving me such confidence and setting me free to be a sheep—a needy, vulnerable, devoted sheep! I want that for you too.

You'll discover that Psalm 23 is a spiritual lullaby that your Shepherd sings over you in every season of your life. And it's not just a psalm that gives you comfort in death. Sister, it is a psalm designed to give you confidence in life.

So, here's how we'll do this thing: you spend time with your Shepherd during the week doing the daily work. There are only four structured days. The fifth day is a Green Pasture Day—you will love it. Your group will gather seven times. At each session, you'll say hey to your Bible study buddies, your leader will welcome you, and you'll begin with prayer. Then you'll let me join you through the video.

I hope our time together will challenge you, comfort you, and clarify something about God or yourself that will help you know Him better and love Him more. After the video, your group will talk through what you've discovered in your week of private study. You'll find suggested questions on the group guide for each week. If you are the awesome woman leading this group, you'll find hints and helps in the back of this book.

OK, last two things just for you. I put together a *Psalm 23* playlist you will want to listen to as you go through this psalm. It is at JenniferRothschild.com/Psalm23. While you're there, you will also find my weekly video teaching summaries. That way, if you miss a video, you won't miss out on any part of this *Psalm 23* experience.

Sister, you have been on my heart the whole time I have been writing this study. I'm honored to share these truths I've learned (and am still learning) with you, and I'm praying you and your Shepherd will grow even closer as you spend time in this psalm.

Well, that's all from me! Let's do this, sister!

Love,

Jennifer

GROUP SESSION 1

Rather than a formal leader guide in the back, we've provided what we hope is a simple and functional group plan on these pages with an additional word to leaders in the back. Each week will begin with a two-page group guide like this. I suggest that you divide your group time into three parts: 1. Welcome and prayer; 2. Watch the video; 3. Group discussion of the personal study for the past week and the video you've just watched.

    The session guide for this first meeting is for us to get to know each other. Then we'll each go do our personal study. (It will be fun, I promise.) Each day, plan to spend a few minutes with that day's study. Don't worry if some days you don't get it all. This isn't a race, and you can come back later. When we meet next group session, we'll have this week's study to discuss. Now let's get to know each other, and I'll join you by way of video.

BEFORE THE VIDEO

Welcome and Prayer

VIDEO NOTES

David, the shepherd who became a king, wrote this psalm about the King who was his _____.

Most scholars believe David wrote Psalm 23 when he was _____. *[handwritten: wrote when he was older]*

Psalm 23 was written because we are like _____ and _____ need a _____.

David knew in every season he was _____ with his Shepherd.

It is with our Shepherd where we _____ our _____.

Four Fears Jesus Knows We May Have

1. We may not fear death itself because of our faith, but we still can _____ the _____. We may fear people who _____ us.

2. We may fear being _____, _____, or _____.

3. We may fear we won't have _____ _____. We may worry about _____ things.

4. We may fear we are not _____ and _____ by God.

God's goodness toward us has _____ to do with our greatness.

CONVERSATION GUIDE

Video 1 and Getting to Know Each Other

What is one thing you want this group to know about you?

What drew you to this study of Psalm 23?

What emotions, memories, or thoughts come to mind when you read Psalm 23?

Are there times in your life when you don't feel safe, physically or emotionally? Explain.

Do you currently feel safe with your Shepherd? Why or why not?

What do you hope to gain from this study?

> Would you like to read my written summary of this video teaching? Just go to jenniferrothschild.com/psalm23.

YOUR SHEPHERD'S GOT YOUR BACK

The LORD is my shepherd;
I shall not want.

PSALM 23:1

#PSALM23STUDY

DAY 1

I'm sitting here with my coffee thinking of you.

I wonder where you are right now as you open this book. I wonder how your heart is. I've written several Bible studies, but there is something that feels so uniquely personal, so intimate, about this one. I feel like we're walking the same paths, dealing with the same challenges, fighting the same fears, and holding on to the same hope.

I imagine you sitting at my kitchen table with me as I write this and sip my coffee—as if we're talking it through, learning from each other. By the way, I'm sure my table has the remains of breakfast stuck to it, so just wipe it with your sleeve. I won't notice, promise!

Oh yeah, I guess I should clarify something right up front. I won't see you wipe away the sticky stuff from my table because I'm blind. If this is the first time we've done Bible study together, you may not know I lost most of my sight as a teenager because of a disease called retinitis pigmentosa. It's a degenerative disease. It started with legal blindness and just got darker and darker from there. Now over thirty years later, I've lived in physical darkness longer than I lived in physical light.

So I'm typing this on a laptop that talks, and I'm thankful for the sighted people who will clean this up, edit it, and make it easier for you to read. Girl, it may sound good, but it sure doesn't look pretty when I'm done with it. Blindness has helped me lean hard on the Lord. And, the older I get, the more I understand how much I need to lean on Him, my Shepherd.

Check page 204 in the back of the book to find a list of resources for studying the Bible, including some of my online favorites.

So pour your coffee, tea, or Diet Coke®, open your Bible, and let's get started.

Read Psalm 23 out loud. You can use whichever Bible translation you prefer. You can also go to your favorite Bible website and read it from several versions.

Beautiful, isn't it?

Now before we even study the Scripture, let's study our hearts.

Do any special memories come up when you read, hear, or think of Psalm 23?

What kinds of feelings stir in your heart when you read this passage? Write down some adjectives (*comforted, grateful, lacking, or lonely, for example*).

This passage stirs up all sorts of emotions, doesn't it? Most of us have some memory of Psalm 23 in our past. Maybe it was Granny's favorite psalm. Maybe it was read at the funeral of someone you love. Or maybe you saw it on a plaque or memorized it as a child.

Psalm 23 is personal. It's not an arm's-length, past-tense, wouldn't-it-be-nice kind of passage.

Psalm 23 is a right here, right now, up close passage about you and your Shepherd.

So let's personalize it! Fill in our adapted Psalm 23 below with your name, and then read it out loud again. Once you've filled in each blank, consider taking a picture of it with your phone so you can be reminded all day long that your Shepherd is with you (because most of us have our phones with us all the time).

PSALM 23

The LORD is _____ shepherd;

she shall not want.

He makes _____ to lie down in green pastures;

He leads _____ beside the still waters.

He restores _____ soul;

He leads _____ in the paths of righteousness

For His name's sake.

Yea, though _____ walks through the valley

  of the shadow of death,

she will fear no evil;

For her Shepherd is with her;

His rod and His staff, they comfort _____.

The shepherd prepares a table before _____

  in the presence of her enemies;

He anoints _____ head with oil;

her cup runs over.

Surely goodness and mercy shall follow _____

All the days of her life;

And _____ will dwell in the house of the LORD

Forever.

Psalm 23

THE LORD IS MY SHEPHERD

OK, now let's study the Scripture.

The first four words of Psalm 23 are the perfect launching pad for understanding this psalm. David, who wrote this psalm, tells us "The LORD is my … ," and then he finishes with "shepherd." But "shepherd" is just one way to illustrate God's character.

> There are many verses in the Bible that describe who God is. Go to your favorite online Bible study resource or to Google®, and search the Bible for the first four words in this verse—*The LORD is my*. Then, list some of the verses you found below, and fill in the blank with the description. I've included a few Scripture starters to get you going.

Psalm 16:5   The LORD is my _____.

Psalm 18:2   The LORD is my _____.

Psalm 27:1   The LORD is my _____.

Psalm 28:7   The LORD is my _____.

_____   The LORD is my _____.

_____   The LORD is my _____.

_____   The LORD is my _____.

_____   The LORD is my _____.

God is so many things to us: our portion, our cup of blessing, our rock and fortress, to name just a few.

But the word *our* isn't in any of those verses, is it? Think about the word *my*. The verse doesn't say that the Lord is *a* shepherd or *our* shepherd. It says He is *my* shepherd just as the other Scriptures you found state that He is *my* portion, *my* rock, and so forth.

> What does the word *my* in this context mean to you?

To me, *my* means personal possession. Just ask any toddler. *My* means that toy belongs to *me*. It is covered with my drool, practically crushed in my little fist, and treasured and valued as if it is the only toy in the toy box. It is my personal possession.

When Scripture tells you that the LORD is your portion, your cup of blessing, your shepherd, your rock, your salvation, and your fortress—Scripture is shouting the truth with the intensity of a 3-year-old—*the LORD is mine!* My light, my rock, my portion, my shepherd. Mine.

I love that. Who He is, is personal to you.

David talks about God as if God belonged to him and he belonged to God. In other words, the relationship is intimate, safe, and permanent.

> Do you, like David, talk about God as if He belongs to you and you belong to Him? Is God personal to you? How do you describe your relationship with God?

If you wouldn't describe your relationship as intimate, safe, and permanent, like David did, sister, my prayer for you is that by the time we've walked this path together, you will. The truth is, if you know Christ, you are your Beloved's and He is yours (Song of Sol. 6:3).

In David's day and culture, it was all about community. Individualism was not the thing like it is here in this day and age. Sheep were never in the pasture alone. They were always in a flock. So for David to write this psalm in his culture and day, as a singular individual when comparing himself to a sheep, spoke to his great value. It speaks to your great value and my great value also.

Put down your pen for just a minute and ponder that. Picture that.

It's like being on a crowded dance floor and the only person you are aware of, the only one who exists at that very moment, is the one who holds you in his arms, the partner who dances with you. That is how it is with your Shepherd. In this crowded world where you're pulled back and forth, caught in the bustle, hearing competing voices, your Shepherd has you. He has your back. He holds you. He guides you. He will not let you go.

He is with you.

I know this may sound weird, but even though I'm blind, I remember and understand concepts better as pictures. When it comes to this psalm, I see in my mind's eye a strong shepherd and a little lamb. But to really personalize it, I imagine a strong and gentle dance partner who leads me each step. As I follow him, I can relax and enjoy the music. I feel free and safe.

Can you think of another picture that may help you really get the feel of how personal and intimate this psalm is? If so, jot it down. Or if you're artsy, draw it!

Review the list of Scriptures describing who God is that you completed earlier (see p. 13). Consider and jot down how those qualities of God's character are personal to you.

How does each quality of God's character show up in your life? How do these qualities make you feel safe? How do they affirm that you are not alone?

Oh sister, when I think of God as my rock, I think of how He stabilizes me and grounds me when life feels so shaky. When I consider how the LORD is my portion, I see in all the areas of my life where I feel insufficient or weak, He is enough, all I need. And when I think of the LORD as my Shepherd, I feel safe with Him. I see how He has guided me through green pastures and dark valleys. To be honest, when I really lean on Him as my Shepherd, I feel the freedom to be as needy and dependent as a sheep. I want that for you, too, my friend.

Well, I'm out of coffee, and I guess I should clean the table! We'll stop right here. Just spend the rest of your day meditating on the Lord as your Shepherd. Be needy. Be vulnerable. Be carried. Be loved. Be led.

Be you. And He will be your Shepherd.

DAY 2

Hey, girl! After your study yesterday, did you experience a deeper awareness of your Shepherd's presence? Was it more personal to you? Did you sense that He was truly with you? I hope so. That's been one of the sweetest blessings for me as I've studied Psalm 23.

Sometimes our lives can feel lonely. Not always because we're alone but because we feel isolated in our own situations. We feel left on our own when it comes to carrying our burdens or navigating the demands of our world.

Loneliness is one of the hardest parts of blindness. It's not because I don't have people! Girl, I've got my people! I love my friends and family who make my life so rich. And, look, now you are one of them, you're right here doing this study with me!

No, this loneliness comes from living in my darkness by myself, being isolated in its invisible, impenetrable walls. Blindness sequesters me from the intimacy of reading a million words in my husband's eyes, sharing the wonder of viewing a mountain range with other tourists, or experiencing the intuitive knowing that comes from a facial expression.

I'm sure you've got your thing that can make you feel alone too. It might be anxiety or divorce or illness or fear. Regardless of your situation, the Shepherd knows and enters in fully present with you.

We are not alone because He is our very own.

Before we study the Scripture, let's study our hearts.

> Is there an area of your life in which you feel alone? Feel free to write it into a prayer. If you don't want to write it out, just sit with your Shepherd and tell Him. Ask Him to enter into your lonely place and reassure you of His presence.

THE WHO, WHEN, AND WHY OF PSALM 23

The shepherd who became king wrote this psalm about the King who was his Shepherd.

David grew up a shepherd and became a giant-slaying singer and songwriter. He was called "a man after [God's] own heart (1 Sam. 13:14).

Around 1005 BC, David became the king of Judah (2 Sam. 2:4; 5:3) and died around 965 BC.[1] Most scholars think he wrote Psalm 23 near the end of his life. After all, it does have a "looking back" feel. He had experienced times of peace and rest (Ps. 23:2). He'd been through some dark, life-threatening times (v. 4). He had lived long enough to make a few enemies (v. 5), and he'd also enjoyed plenty of prosperity (v. 6).

In fact, some scholars believe David wrote Psalm 23 when he was on the run, held up at Mahanaim (2 Sam. 17:24) during the civil war brought on by his son Absalom's rebellion (2 Sam. 15–17).

We don't know exactly when or where the psalm was written. But we do know "whatever was written in earlier times was written for our instruction, so that through perseverance and the encouragement of the Scriptures we might have hope" (Rom. 15:4, NASB).

MY SHEPHERD

Now, let's study the Scripture. Pour your coffee or tea, if you haven't yet. (I'm on my second cup.) Here we go!

Since David sets up this whole psalm based on God being our Shepherd, let's make sure we understand the nature and job of a shepherd.

Search your Bible concordance or online resource to discover if God is referred to as a shepherd anywhere else in the Old Testament. Check in the New Testament, too, to see if Jesus is called a Shepherd. You'll discover that prophets, overseers, and the coming Messiah are also called shepherds.

Based on what you find, use the two columns on the opposite page to jot down what each verse suggests about the actions of a shepherd. I've included some Scripture starters again for you.

REFERENCE	THE SHEPHERD'S ACTIONS
Psalm 28:9	
Psalm 80:1	
Isaiah 40:11	
Jeremiah 31:10	
Micah 7:14	
John 10:11-15	
1 Peter 2:25	
1 Peter 5:4	

Read through the actions of a shepherd that you listed in the second column.

> What do those actions suggest about a shepherd's character? Here's a fun way to answer. Pretend you and I just had coffee with a local shepherd. (Not likely, but go with it.) Describe him to our imaginary single girlfriend who has been searching on "SingleShepherd.com" for just the right guy!

If I were to help you and our shepherd friend out by writing a profile for him on "SingleShepherd.com," it would read:

Strong but gentle man who isn't afraid to fight bears and lions. Prone to patience with a protective nature. Observant with great management skills and an excellent provider. Willing to sacrifice and serve. Gets great satisfaction from helping, blessing, and guiding others. Faithful to the end.

OK, what woman wouldn't want all that?

You have all that, and more, in your Shepherd.

The Lord is your Shepherd. That means, your Shepherd tends to your needs.

He carries you when you can't carry on. He stands with you and stands up for you when enemies stand against you. He protects you when you're unsure or feel unsafe.

He leads you when you don't know which way to go. He saves you from your sin and yourself.

He keeps you close to Him, and He is faithful to you forever.

I think we just need to stop and thank Him for being our Shepherd, don't you? Let's lay down our mugs and pens and fears and worries and anything else that is in our hands or on our hearts and sit with our Shepherd.

Want to borrow one of my favorite psalms of thanksgiving? Here are three that I reference and pray often:

Psalm 100 • Psalm 107 • Psalm 138

Tell Him how grateful we are that He is with us and for us. Select a psalm of thanksgiving to pray to Him. Take your time, sister. Linger and breathe. Rest in His presence.

Now, back to our study! When David wrote Psalm 23, he knew exactly the character and nature of a shepherd because he had been one. He knew what kind of man it took to manage sheep in the countryside of Israel.

Early in the morning, he would have led the flock out from the fold, guiding the sheep to pasture. He would have watched and tended them all day, making sure no sheep wandered off and that each sheep was safe from predators. And, if one of the little flock got lost, he would diligently seek that sheep until she was found. Under the blistering sun, he'd lead the sheep to water—but not just any water. He would lead them to still waters since sheep won't drink if the water moves too fast.

At night, he would bring the whole flock back home to the fold, counting each one as she passed under his rod. Then he had to stay alert to guard the sheep from wild animals who had an appetite for lamb chops! That's just a city girl summary of a shepherd's day.

But with that in mind, look at what Scripture tells us about our Shepherd— our Good Shepherd, Jesus. Read John 10:1-15. Jot down the reference or write out the verse that corresponds with each quality of a shepherd listed below. Then, finish the "My Shepherd" sentence below each quality, to describe how the Shepherd has acted in this way on your behalf.

The shepherd names his sheep. Reference: _____

My Shepherd gives me a name; He calls me _____.

The shepherd leads his sheep. Reference: _____

My Shepherd leads me to _____.

The shepherd gives his life for his sheep. Reference: _____

My Shepherd has sacrificed for me by _____.

The shepherd protects his sheep. Reference: _____

My Shepherd protects me from _____.

The shepherd knows his sheep. Reference: _____

My Shepherd knows me; He knows I _____.

Oh my friend, the Lord is your Shepherd who leads you, provides for you, and protects you. Jesus is your Good Shepherd who gives His very life for you, His sheep.

Well, I guess we need to quit for now since our mugs are empty and our hearts are full!

Find one statement or Scripture from today that ministered to you and write it on a sticky note, index card, or type it into your phone. Think about it throughout your day as you walk with your Shepherd.

DAY 3

I'm so glad you're back, I saved you a seat at my table because I want to start with a fun question. What animal are you most like? Or, if you could pick an animal to be, which one would you choose and why?

If you're on Twitter®, I'd love for you to let me know your answer! (I'm @JennRothschild!)

I know, I should have warned you that we were starting a little differently today. But I've done some thinking about this. If I could be any animal, I would be an elephant. Why? Well, they have really big brains, and they never forget anything. (I could use both of those qualities about now.) Also, they are loyal to their herds. They like to play. They are gentle but can take care of themselves. And, when you're an elephant, being all leathery and wrinkled and gaining weight are just no big deal!

But the animal I am most like? I wouldn't have answered this way before I studied Psalm 23, but now I know. I am most like a sheep.

You are too. We have a lot in common with those woolly, wonderful creatures.

THE NATURE OF A SHEEP

So let's open the Word and see what it says about us being sheep. Pour your coffee, open your concordance, or go online to your favorite Bible resource to find references in the Bible that compare us to sheep. I've listed some Scripture starters to get you going.

Next to each reference note what the verse says or suggests about the nature of sheep.

SHEEP SCRIPTURES	SHEEP NATURE
Psalm 79:13	
Psalm 95:7	
Psalm 100:3	
Isaiah 53:6	
John 10:1-16	
Hebrews 13:20	

Use the verses above, or find more verses in both the Old and New Testaments that confirm the following descriptions of sheep. Write the references in the appropriate categories on the next page.

THE RÉSUMÉ OF A SHEEP

1. SHEEP GO ASTRAY.

2. SHEEP NEED GUIDANCE.

3. SHEEP ARE VULNERABLE.

4. SHEEP ARE VALUABLE.

Do any of those qualities of sheep feel familiar to you? Oh girl, that could be my own résumé, especially the first three. I easily stray from the grace of the Lord and try to do things on my own. I'm desperate for guidance. Without God's Word and His people, I can easily start to think I know the way, the only way—my way, the best way!

I am far more emotionally vulnerable than I want to admit, and I'm still learning that I really am valuable to God. I am so like a sheep, as are you. So make this résumé your own.

1. SHEEP GO ASTRAY.

Times I have gone astray:

No matter where you've strayed, your Shepherd says to you what He said to Israel so many years ago. Read Deuteronomy 30:3-10, and notice how many times God uses words such as *bring back* or *restore*. Sister, you never go so far that your Shepherd won't restore you and return you to His Side.

2. SHEEP NEED GUIDANCE.

Situations in which I needed guidance:

You can ask your Shepherd for guidance just like the psalmists did. Pray Psalm 25:4-5 and Psalm 143:8-10. Your Shepherd will always lovingly lead you.

3. SHEEP ARE VULNERABLE.

Seasons or circumstances when I felt vulnerable:

When you feel unsafe and need protection, use Psalm 71 to declare that your Shepherd has your back—because He does and always will.

4. SHEEP ARE VALUABLE.

What makes me feel valued and valuable to my Shepherd:

When you feel overlooked or undervalued, see your value through your Shepherd's eyes by meditating on Psalm 139.

OK girl, what do you think? What animal are you most like? Do sheep now rank right up there at the top of your list? Are you OK with being a sheep?

Sometimes we don't like to think of ourselves as sheep because we don't like to admit we're vulnerable, needy, or capable of straying. Is that you? Or maybe you haven't been able to admit you are like a sheep because you just can't grasp how valuable you are to the Shepherd—that He would leave the ninety-nine just to come find you and bring you to His side (Luke 15:1-7).

Take a minute to pause and reflect on this. You won't experience all the Lord can be and wants to be as your Shepherd if you aren't willing to be a sheep.

Read 1 Peter 5:7, and do these three things:

1. **BELIEVE WHAT IT SAYS!** Trust the truth that He cares for you. He doesn't just care about you as one puny sheep in a big flock. He actually cares specifically for you. Just as a shepherd takes care of his sheep, your Shepherd wants to take care of you. Can you trust that truth today?

2. **DO WHAT IT SAYS!** Seriously, cast your cares upon your Shepherd. He tells you to. He wants you to. What would that look like in your life if you really did that today? If you truly cast your cares on Him? Think of just one care or concern. Imagine it in your hands. Name it. Then, imagine shifting it from your hands to your Shepherd's shoulders. Now, leave it there. He can carry it better than you. That's what sheep do— they trust the shepherd and expect him to care for them and about them.

3. **PRAY WHAT IT SAYS!** Based on 1 Peter 5:7, write a prayer to your Shepherd asking Him to reveal His care for you in ways you can recognize. Ask Him to help you cast (and keep casting) your cares on Him. Thank Him for caring about what you care about. What matters to you matters to your Shepherd.

I'm so grateful God cares about and for us, His sheep, aren't you? We really do have so much in common with woolly animals. But you know, there is one thing that we do not have in common with sheep—well, besides the fact that we don't eat grass, we have larger vocabularies, and our hair isn't nearly as itchy—we aren't always honest.

Sheep are honest creatures. If they are lost and afraid, they don't fake it. They bleat and shiver with fear, waiting for their shepherd to rescue them. If sheep feel unsafe or vulnerable, they don't puff their little chests out and act tough. No, they get closer to each other and the shepherd because they know they can't defend themselves. They don't try to be something they're not. Do you?

I'm learning how much I really am like a sheep, and I'm OK with that. Even though I try to have it all together, to always be strong and brave, at times, in the deepest part of me I'm fearful, vulnerable, and weak. I long for someone to be stronger and smarter than me. I wish I really felt as confident as I sometimes seem. Deep down, I just want to relax into whatever I face knowing I don't face it alone and I don't have to be in charge. I really don't want to have to hold it all together. Deep down, I just want to be held. How about you?

Oh my friend, it is OK to be a sheep. Of all the comparisons God could have made, He chose the image of a needy sheep and a strong, gentle shepherd. He's OK with you being a sheep. He loves you just the way you are.

He created you to need Him and to have your needs met by Him.

And He created you to need other sheep. So if you're studying this with a group (and I sure hope you are), be real with your Bible study buddies. You aren't the only one who feels the way you do. I promise.

Before I studied Psalm 23—or really, before Psalm 23 studied me—I thought I needed to be in control, when I actually needed to be cared for by my Shepherd. I thought I needed to be brave, when I really needed most to be held.

You may think you need to be in control, when what you really need is to be under God's care.

Do you recognize your true nature and admit your true needs?

Think about that today as you walk with your Shepherd. Tomorrow we'll see that when we admit we have nothing, we see we lack nothing.

Hey, my fellow lamb! I'm thinking about my day as I sit at my computer writing this. My mind wanders to all I need to get done today, and I'm trying to plan how I will fit it all in! You know how that goes, right? I know you do.

But as I was thinking about my list, I then thought, *Sheep don't have daily planners. Sheep have daily needs.* Hmmm.

Sheep wake up in the morning with probably just a few things on their simple minds. First, food! Second, who will get me food? Third? Ah yes, the shepherd. He will make sure I have food. Right?

So as we sit here together now, I'm trashing my to-do list and focusing on my Shepherd, not my needs.

Can you do that too? He cares about us and for us so we can cast our cares on Him right here, right now. If you need to pause and do that, take a minute to refocus in prayer.

Lord, help us to focus on You. Show us truth today. In Jesus' name, amen.

I SHALL NOT WANT

Let's go back to the sheep's daily needs for a moment. Sheep learn to associate the shepherd with their needs being met. When that happens, the shepherd becomes their focus, not their needs. They "shall not want"—not because they have an all-you-can-eat buffet set before them, but because they have their shepherd with them.

It is the same with us. We shall not want because we have all we need in our Shepherd.

> So let's study this! Go to your favorite Bible study reference or online resource and find parallel versions of Psalm 23:1. Write below the different ways "I shall not want" is translated.

The Message paraphrases "I shall not want" into "I don't need a thing." I love that. The New International Version translates it as, "I lack nothing." That word *lack* shows up in other places in Scripture too.

> Google, search on an online Bible study resource, or look in your concordance for instances where *lack* appears in Scripture. In the chart below, jot down the references that you find. Beside each reference, write how *lack* or *lacking nothing* is used in the passage and how it applies to you. (You may need to look at different translations of each reference to find the actual word *lack*. Some translations will use a synonym.)

WHAT IS A PARALLEL VERSION?

It is a different translation of the same text. For example, the New King James Version translates Psalm 23:1b as "I shall not want." While the Christian Standard Bible translates it as "I have what I need." You can find parallel versions in a parallel Bible, on a Bible app such as YouVersion, or in an online resource like Biblehub.com.

REFERENCES	HOW *LACK* OR *LACKING NOTHING* IMPACTS ME
Deuteronomy 2:7	
Psalm 34:9-10	
Proverbs 11:14	
Proverbs 15:22	
Hosea 4:6	

Some Scriptures tell us what happens when we lack knowledge, judgment, or wisdom. And girl, it ain't pretty! Other passages describe how we lack nothing when we seek God or follow Him. And that is beautiful.

> With these Scriptures on your heart, journal your thoughts about what you may lack or think you lack and how it affects your life. Settle back to spend some time with your Shepherd, and listen to His voice.

I think I lack:

I live as if I lack:

I wish I had:

If I only had:

I act like I lack:

I need:

I lack:

Sister, there are no right answers to these journal prompts. We're all going to view this differently based on our current circumstances, our hopes and dreams, and our walks with the Lord. You may even want to use these as prayer prompts.

Sometimes when we think of *lack,* our minds race to physical things such as a car that runs well or a mate (or a mate who behaves well!). And other times, when we think of what we lack, we may think of emotional or spiritual qualities such as wisdom or self-control.

Let's sit on a Judean hill with David and try to get into his shepherd brain to discover what he may have been referencing as he wrote "I lack nothing" (NIV). Read Psalm 23 in its entirety as if David is writing it from a sheep's perspective. As you read, list the need or needs he is likely referring to in each verse.

"The LORD is my Shepherd, I shall not want … "

Verse 2

Verse 3

Verse 4

Verse 5

Verse 6

The psalm lists the following needs that the sheep will not lack: food and drink, tranquility, rescue, guidance, freedom from fear, protection, and the shepherd's presence all the days of their lives. Funny that things like stuff and status didn't make the list. Sister, we may experience lack in this life, but we will only lack what we don't need. We will never lack what we do need.

When our oldest son was about two years old, he'd sprawl his little legs over the armrests of his car seat and call from the back seat of the car, "I need! I need! Mommy, I neeeeeeed!" He never finished the sentence though. When I asked, "What do you need," he would just repeat, "I neeeeed!" That's kind of how we are too. We call to our Shepherd, "I need!" And if He asks, "What do you need that I am not supplying?" We just pause and call out, "I need!"

Like children, like sheep, we aren't always tuned in to our real needs. Here's a prayer I pray often: *Lord, clarify what my needs are so I can see how You meet them.*

Do you need to pause and pray that prayer too? Or maybe you need to jot it on a sticky note and place it somewhere to help hone your spiritual radar.

Read Philippians 4:19. How does God meet our needs? Through whom or what?

Look back over the journal prompts you listed earlier. Keeping in mind that all we truly need is met in and through Christ, our Good Shepherd, and understanding that Fort Knox is like a child's piggy bank compared to His infinite supply, how does Christ Himself meet your needs through His glorious riches or through and in Himself? (If your prompts included spiritual or emotional qualities like wisdom or self-control, find Scriptures that prove how those spiritual needs are met in Christ.)

Girl, we really do lack nothing. Zero. Nada. Nothing! That's a whole lot not to lack, isn't it?

When you looked up *lack*, did you find any New Testament verses where Jesus used the word? If not, go to Google or your Bible resource and search for the word *lack* used with the phrase *one thing*. Write the references you find below.

To whom did Jesus say, "one thing you lack"? (Find Mark 10:17, and look at the subhead or title in your Bible if you need a hint.)

Several Bible versions call the man Jesus encountered "the rich young ruler." I love that. He gets two great adjectives to identify him—rich and young. Wow! For more than two thousand years, he's been rich and young!

You've got some adjectives that identify you too. What are they? Pause for a moment and think about that. Brave, smart mom? Grateful, kind woman? Hardworking, fun wife? Loving, compassionate friend?

Now do more than think about it! Jot down some adjectives below that describe you. And note: you are not allowed to write negative words that reflect your weaknesses. These adjectives must reflect your best, your strengths.

You see, sister, we've got to know our adjectives, what identifies us. Because even though we can pull out some negative words that are true about our weaknesses, there are far more positive words that indicate what we have—our assets, our strengths. When it comes to our strengths, we must be aware of this paradox: our strengths can be the breeding ground for our vulnerabilities.

It can often be our strengths that keep us lacking what we need most.

One of my adjectives is *self-reliant*. It's a good adjective. With my blindness, I developed a relentless can-do attitude which grew into fierce independence. And I guess, because I do have to depend on others so much, being able to pull from my own resources and depend on myself became really important.

So *self-reliant* is truly one of my adjectives. Great strength. But great strengths may put us at great risk.

I've learned that my self-reliance can keep me from being honest and vulnerable. It can cause me to lack humility and build a wall of isolation if I'm not careful.

So if Jesus said to me, "one thing you lack," well, probably, I would think, *Really? Just one thing?* But it would take me back and make me think.

What if Jesus said those words to you?

Ask yourself again, in light of your adjectives, "What do I lack?" Stop, put down your pen, and really ask yourself that question.

What the rich young ruler lacked was directly linked to what he had. Think about what Jesus saw.

> Jesus looked at him and loved him. "One thing you lack," he
> said. "Go, sell everything you have and give to the poor, and
> you will have treasure in heaven. Then come, follow me."
>
> MARK 10:21, NIV

This junior Rockefeller clearly didn't lack money. He didn't lack the desire to do the right things and be the right kind of guy. But what Jesus told him to do exposed what he did lack. He lacked the willingness to let go of his own safety net, his position, and his strengths to depend totally on Jesus for his security and status.

Now, let me make sure I'm clear right here. You don't get treasure in heaven by giving away your TV or tennis shoes.

You get treasure in heaven by making heaven your treasure.

You make Jesus all you need, and then all you need is found in Jesus. In other words, like sheep, you pay more attention to the Shepherd who supplies your needs than you do to the needs themselves. You want your Shepherd more than you want what you want! You put your daily agenda under your Shepherd's authority. You stay with Him, go where He leads, do what He says, and experience "I shall not want" every single day of your life.

Oh girl, I want that so badly, don't you?

Last item for today—"one thing" we lack is important to really consider. But there are four other "one thing" Scriptures that help me see what I have and can have in my Shepherd.

> They're found in Psalm 27:4; Luke 10:41-42; John 9:25; and Philippians 3:13. Look each one up, read the verse in its context, and then place each reference under the correct heading below. Then, personalize each verse by declaring it as a prayer, a praise, or a confession to your Shepherd.

> "One thing is necessary."

> Reference: Prayer:

"One thing I ask."

Reference: Prayer:

"One thing I do."

Reference: Prayer:

"One thing I know."

Reference: Prayer:

We really do lack nothing. However, sometimes we focus on other things or the wrong things, and our misaligned focus keeps us from seeing that we have everything.

David, in Psalm 27, shows us that there is no thing more satisfying than the "one thing" of being with and knowing our Shepherd.

Martha, in Luke 10, reminds us that urgent things are never more important than the "one thing" of just being with, sitting with, our Shepherd.

Paul, in Philippians 3, encourages us that the "one thing" of knowing our Shepherd will always exceed all the awesome things we accomplish in our lives.

And finally, the blind man, in John 9, illustrates that we don't need to understand everything, we just need to know the "one thing" that "though I was blind, now I see!" (v. 25).

Hallelujah!

See sister? We truly lack nothing. Even me, with these blind eyes, I can see that I lack nothing.

Oh Jesus, thank You for being our Shepherd. We shall not want.

WHAT IS A GREEN PASTURE DAY?

When sheep are in a lush pasture, they'll chew their cud and graze for hours, overeating if the shepherd lets them. So the shepherd makes them lie down in the green pasture so they can digest what they've eaten. A green pasture is the place sheep rest and digest.

Psalm 23 is a lush pasture of wisdom and practical truth. We need time to rest in it and digest all we've taken in.

So for each verse (and each week), we will enjoy a Green Pasture Day—a day to just rest and digest.

OK, wow. My heart is full. There's so much to take in from this short verse in Psalm 23. So tomorrow we will have a Green Pasture Day. The sheep needed it and so do we. I'm closing the laptop and going to look at my to-do list. If I forget something important, I'll just explain that I was with you and sheep don't wear watches.

See you in the green pasture, friend!

DAY 5

GREEN PASTURE DAY: A DAY TO REST AND DIGEST

The LORD is my shepherd; I shall not want.

PSALM 23:1

Remember those adjectives that you used to describe yourself yesterday? I bet yours were different from your Bible study buddy's adjectives. It's a great reminder that we are all unique—which means that "rest and digest" may look differently for each one of us. On Green Pasture Days, you'll find a few different options for digesting what you've learned during the week. I'll provide several prompts below, and then you pick and choose what works best for you.

OK, sister, it's time for you to just be with your Shepherd. Use this time to do what you most like to do when you want to remember what God is teaching you. Journal. Draw. Write. Sing. Meditate. Thank the Lord for being your Shepherd.

Here are some things to consider as you rest and digest:

What I loved about Psalm 23:1:

What I learned about my Shepherd from Psalm 23:1:

What I learned about myself from Psalm 23:1:

How I'll live based on what I learned in Psalm 23:1:

Scriptures I want to remember from this week:

Quotes I liked from this week:

Thank You, Lord, for being my
Shepherd. I lack nothing.

To help you meditate on the truths of Psalm 23, I've put together a playlist for each verse of the psalm. You'll find it at jenniferrothschild.com/psalm23. Don't worry, it's free! As you listen to the lyrics of the different songs each week, let them give voice to your prayers and draw you closer to your Shepherd.

GROUP SESSION 2

BEFORE THE VIDEO

Welcome and Prayer

VIDEO NOTES

Verse one of Psalm 23 is David's _____ _____.

The early church embraced the idea of God as our _____.

The shepherd is both _____ and _____. The shepherd is _____ and _____. The shepherd not only _____ _____ his sheep. He _____ _____ his sheep.

Things We Know About Sheep

1. Sheep are easily _____.

2. Sheep are _____.

3. Sheep are _____.

Our Shepherd is the _____ of _____.

Our Shepherd not only _____ us the _____. Our Shepherd _____ the _____.

Three Reasons Why We May Feel Lack

1. We misunderstand our _____ _____.

2. We _____ the _____.

- The thing that we wish God would take away could be the very thing He is using
  to _____ our _____.

3. We mistake the _____.

CONVERSATION GUIDE

Video 2

DAY 1: What characteristic of God is most meaningful to you? Why?
What is comforting and encouraging to you about God being your Shepherd?

DAY 2: How do you experience the Shepherd's care on a daily basis?

DAY 3: How are you most like a sheep?
Is it difficult for you to recognize your true nature and admit your true needs?
Explain.

DAY 4: Are you content? Why or why not?
How does what we lack and what we think we lack drive the way we live our lives
and relate to Christ?
What adjectives identify you?
How can our strengths keep us lacking what we need most?

DAY 5: Share some highlights from your Green Pasture Day.
What is one significant truth you take away from this week of study?

Do you know someone who would be encouraged by this video teaching?
Get my written summary at jenniferrothschild.com/psalm23.

WEEK 2

YOUR SHEPHERD GIVES YOU REST

He makes me to lie down in green pastures; He leads me beside the still waters.

PSALM 23:2

DAY 1

Today I'm sitting by my fireplace with my laptop balanced on my knees. So pull up a chair, I've saved you a seat!

Before we begin studying this beautiful verse, read through Psalm 23 again. As you do, notice again how personal and caring your Shepherd is. Verse 2 gives us the first two specific examples of how our Shepherd takes care of us, His sheep. Write the verse below, pausing with each word. As you linger over each word, think about what that word means, because this week, we're going to pull this verse apart and get the most out of every syllable.

HE MAKES ME TO LIE DOWN

Sitting by the fire is so beautiful, isn't it? It's the perfect place to study what it means to lie down, to rest in green pastures. In fact, I also have a mug of coffee perched on the table beside me because all this tranquility can make a girl drowsy.

So pour your coffee or tea, and let's start with Google, or "The Google" as my not-so-hip brother calls it! Use Google, or your favorite search engine, to search for the words *lie down* along with your favorite online resource name (see the callout for an example).

ONLINE SEARCH HOW-TO

When doing an online search, make sure you type keywords in quotation marks so that the search engine looks for the phrase and not the individual words. You should type something like this in your search bar: "lie down" Bible Gateway. Then, your search results will include individual links to BibleGateway.com, all linking to a verse in the Bible that includes the phrase *lie down*.

If you're not able to do an online search, I've listed some Scripture starters for you that will do the trick.

Next to each reference, paraphrase the specific verse in your own words as a personal "I can rest, because" statement.

REFERENCES	WHY I CAN REST
Psalm 3:5	
Psalm 4:8	
Proverbs 3:23-26	

Did you detect a theme in the verses containing the words *lie down*? The Scripture starters I included showed me I can rest because I'm safe, at peace, and confident in God. That makes sense. It's hard to lie down anywhere if you feel afraid or don't feel safe.

Consider some of those fearful or unsafe situations. Maybe it's a hotel room where you're not confident about the security. Or perhaps you struggle to doze on the beach because you're afraid some distracted, swimsuit clad tourist will step on your head!

Name other situations where you can't easily rest.

Why did you select these situations?

We may name all different kinds of places and situations, but what they have in common is that we don't feel enough peace, safety, or confidence to just let down our guards and rest.

Remember what it felt like to be a little girl in the back seat of the car when your parents or the grown-ups you trusted were driving? You didn't hesitate to lie down in the back seat and fall asleep while you were being driven home. (This was pre-car seat days, of course!) It was easy to rest because you felt safe and protected—the grown-ups who drove were your confidence. You intuitively knew they would get you home.

Girl, it's the same with your Shepherd. You can trust Him and rest in Him, knowing He's got you.

SAFE WITH YOUR SHEPHERD

Sheep can lie down and rest no matter where they are when they feel safe with their shepherd. You and I need to be reminded that we are safe with our Shepherd, too, no matter what situations we find ourselves in.

Let's find Scripture that affirms we are safe in Him, truth that affirms we can lie down and rest in the back seat knowing He's got the wheel. Look in your concordance, or do an online word search for words like *hide, shelter,* and *protect*—words that represent safety to you. I'll share some of mine.

Based on each verse, what can you know about your Shepherd that affirms you are safe, safe enough to rest?

SAFE SCRIPTURES	SAFETY AFFIRMATIONS
Psalm 27:5	
Psalm 32:7-8	
Psalm 91:1-4	
Isaiah 25:4	

Knowing God will shelter me when I'm in trouble, knowing there are songs of deliverance being sung over me even when I can't hear them, knowing when it's dark there is a greater shadow of God's wings sheltering me, and knowing that when I feel the most helpless my Shepherd is my defender—these kinds of truths give me a sense of rest and assurance when I feel vulnerable.

And talk about feeling vulnerable. Girl, with blindness, I've got tons of reasons to feel unsure and unsafe. In fact, I got confused and disoriented in a women's restroom just a few weeks ago, and it really, really bothered me—OK, it freaked me out!

Oh man, I need a sip of coffee before I tell you this story. OK, deep breath. In the bathroom of this trendy restaurant, the stall was at a weird angle and every wall felt like a barn door. So no matter which wall I put my hand on, none made sense. They all felt the same—grooves, slats, bolts, and decorative metal—none felt like the door once I was inside the stall.

I was in the restroom alone. My husband was waiting outside, and there was not another woman in there. (Actually, I'm glad of that. I would have been humiliated!) Getting in was no problem because the stall door swung behind me and evidently clicked itself shut when I went in the stall. But getting out? Well, that was a problem. Where was the latch? Where was the door?

I panicked. I felt an overwhelming dread come over me, not knowing where I was, how I got there, or how I could get out. Phil must have heard me from outside the restroom door. I'm not sure what he heard. Maybe it was a strange banging and clawing coming from the stall. He poked his head in and asked, "Honey, are you OK?" I'm not sure what I said, but it was obvious to him that I was not OK. So he marched right into that women's restroom and knocked on the outside of the stall door so I could find it.

When I pulled the latch and opened that door, I was fighting back anxiety and fear. I just wanted out of there. He asked me what happened. I tried to explain, but I couldn't because really I didn't know. All I knew was I felt stuck, afraid, confused, and vulnerable. Let's just say, there was no rest in that restroom!

We just cannot rest—we can't be at peace—if we don't feel safe.

We need to find our safety in our Shepherd not in our situations.

Now girl, that previous statement is easy to say but not always easy to do. Even though I knew in my brain that I was safe, safe with my Shepherd in that restroom stall, my racing heart was not at rest. It clearly hadn't read the memo! I share this with you because we've all got our stuff that makes us feel unsafe—relationships, situations, places, and even memories. But for those of us who know Christ, we have a Shepherd in whom we can hide and be sheltered. When we do, we are safe enough to rest.

> What relationships, situations, places, or memories tense you up or freak you out? In which areas of your life do you find it hard to lower your guard and rest in the security you have in your Shepherd? Write out your thoughts here. If you don't feel comfortable writing your response, just sit with your Shepherd and pray about it.

Now write out a prayer to your Shepherd, asking Him to assure you that you are safe in Him when it comes to those areas you listed. Finish your time by praying one of the Safe Scriptures you listed earlier that help you know you are safe with your Shepherd.

Oh Lord, my Shepherd,

Amen.

Fear will always lie to you and tell you that you aren't safe and you can't trust your Shepherd. Insecurity will tell you that you will never find peace and you've got to keep your guard up. Fear is a liar. Insecurity is not your friend. So choose one of the Safe Scriptures from today to meditate on and memorize. That's what I do—I meditate on God's promises that remind me I am safe with my Shepherd. The more we do this, the sooner our racing hearts will get the memo!

Which verse will you meditate on and memorize?

Oh my friend, your life may not feel like an inviting green pasture all the time, but you can still lie down and rest. And you can live restfully.

It's not our situations that make us safe enough to rest; it is our Shepherd who makes us safe enough to rest.

Thank You, Lord, for being our Shepherd. We love you. Amen.

OK, sister, we're done for the day! I'm praying that God takes His Word and what you've pondered today and sinks it deep into your heart so you know how very safe you are in Him. Peace to you.

DAY 2

Hey there! Let's jump right in. A good way to study Scripture is to read a verse several times and pick out some of the parts of speech. You know, like you did in eighth grade? Don't panic if you're not a grammar girl. This will be easy, and I'll walk you through it.

> We'll start with verbs, also known as action words. Find the verbs in Psalm 23:2, and circle them in your Bible. Or, jot down the entire verse below, and circle the verbs.

Just in case grammar makes you break out in cold sweats, here are the verbs: *makes (lets)* and *leads*.

> Now think about those verbs. Who is doing the action?

> What does that suggest about God's role as the Shepherd and your role as the sheep?

Sheep have one responsibility, and it's not to find the green pasture and still waters. Their one and only responsibility is to obey and follow their shepherd. They don't look for green pastures and still waters, they look to the shepherd. He leads them to green pastures and still waters.

Sheep love green pastures because that's where they are fed and where they get to rest. Tomorrow, we'll get real specific about our own personal green pastures, what feeds us and brings us rest. In the meantime, think about this: Do you spend more time looking for green pastures than you do looking to your Shepherd?

What does Psalm 23:2 suggest about finding the green pastures you're looking for?

NOUN/PRONOUN

A noun is a person, place, or thing. It tells us who is doing the action. A pronoun is a word or phrase that can be substituted for a noun or noun phrase (Example: he, me, she, etc.). It can do everything a noun can do. As you study Scripture, stop to consider who is doing each action mentioned. It will deepen your understanding of the passage and give you a new perspective.

OK, tuck that away in your heart while we move on to the nouns and pronouns. Draw a box around the nouns and pronouns from verse 2 in your Bible or in the verse you may have written out.

If you're still recovering from the verb incident, don't panic, here are the nouns: *pastures, waters.* And the pronouns: *he, me.*

Think about the pronouns in this verse. How many are there and to whom are they referring?

Take a moment to ponder what those pronouns suggest about your relationship with the Shepherd.

Me and He. He and me. (Bad grammar, I know.) But it's all about togetherness. Verse 2 has a companionship feel, doesn't it? It's a picture of *withship*. The shepherd *with* the sheep.

Withship is like a bicycle built for two—you and your Shepherd.

> I really want us to picture this. So even if you are the least artsy woman who ever picked up a pen, draw a bicycle built for two in the space provided. Above each seat on your beautiful bike, write who is sitting in that specific seat—you or the Shepherd.

Where are you sitting? I don't have to see your picture to know that you probably put yourself on the back of the bike because we good, Christian girls know that our assigned seat is in back. But be honest. In reality, are you on the front of the bike, in charge and pedaling hard to get to that green pasture so you can rest?

Or perhaps you're in the right place but with the wrong heart. You're seated on the back of the bike, but constantly shouting directions to your Shepherd and calling it prayer. Do you think you know better than Him where the green pastures in your life should be?

Or are you content to sit on the back of the bike, safe with your Shepherd, knowing He is in total control?

SHEEP FOLLOW WHERE THE SHEPHERD LEADS

Read Psalm 23:2 again. Who is doing the making and the leading?

I know, I know! Not us. We are called to follow.

Following is freeing.

Surrender brings serenity.

If we don't obey or follow our Shepherd, we will never receive the rest we long for.

Sister, we often reduce this beautiful verse to a spiritual spa day! We think it's only about resting and being refreshed. While resting and being refreshed are beautiful benefits, they aren't the main message of this tiny verse. Have you figured out what it is? I'll give you some possible answers. Circle the one you think is the main message:

God's provision   God's authority

God's guidance   God's protection

Oh girl, it's all about God's authority and our surrender.

You see, there is a direct link between our surrender to God and the rest we receive from God. Ponder that statement. Why do you think that's true? As you answer, think about the illustration of being on the back of the bike.

Jesus, our Good Shepherd, teaches us this principle as well. Read Matthew 11:28-29, and jot down the two things He tells us to do in verse 29 to receive rest for our souls:

_____ and _____

WHAT IS A YOKE?

Yoke is not a word we hear very often. But in Jesus' day, those listening to His teaching would have known He was referring to a piece of equipment used by a farmer. The yoke was a wooden beam fastened over the necks of two animals—most often oxen—enabling them to work together to pull loads or plow fields. To better understand its use, do a quick Google search to find an image of a yoke. Makes sense now, right?

What did Jesus mean when He said to take up His yoke? If you're not sure, you can look it up in a Bible dictionary or encyclopedia. (Or you can just check out the info in the box on the left!)

When a Jewish teacher, a Rabbi, used this kind of language, he was saying *follow my teaching, submit to my authority, be my disciple.* The people of Jesus' day were toiling under the burdensome and wearying rabbinical teachings and traditions. Jesus offered them a different way. If they submitted to Him, learned from Him, and allowed Him to be the authority in their lives, they wouldn't be worn out. Rather, their souls would find rest.

Based on what you know about the message and teaching of Jesus, how is that true? How does His yoke bring us rest? Check out the following Scriptures to help answer the question: 2 Corinthians 8:9; Philippians 2:13; Titus 2:11-12; 1 John 5:3.

The yoke of Jesus is one of grace, mercy, love, and forgiveness. It is not based on what I can do but what He has done. When we take Jesus' yoke upon us, we are saying, "Your grace saved me a seat on the back of Your bike. You are in the front seat of this bike, and I will pedal along with You, behind You. I will follow You."

That means, sister, He picks the path. He determines the pace, and He will carry the weight of the journey. If you've ever been on the back of a tandem bike, trust me, the person on the back doesn't even have to pedal if she doesn't want to! *Wink.* The one on the front is doing the bulk of the work. All I have to do when Phil is on the front of our tangerine bicycle built for two is trust him, follow him, and cooperate with him.

Trust and obedience bring us rest.

So if that is true, what is the opposite of trust?

What is the opposite of obedience?

Oh sister, unbelief and rebellion keep us from rest.

Find Hebrews 3:7-19. Most Bibles have a subhead or title above verse 7. Does yours? If so, write what it says.

OK, now read through those thirteen verses. This passage tells us why the people of Israel who came out of Egypt couldn't enter into their rest, which represents the promised land. What was the bottom-line, sum-it-up reason in verse 19?

Look at your own life. Consider the times you feel the least rested in your soul. Is it caused by unbelief? Explain.

For the Israelites, unbelief showed up as rebellion, complaining, and seeking their own way. What does unbelief look like in your life?

I don't want to miss out on rest because of unbelief, and I know you don't either. Girl, we can be so deceived that we think God and His promises can't be trusted or that our plan is better.

So what's one thing that can protect us from being deceived, from wiggling out of our Shepherd's yoke and missing out on His rest? The answer is found in Hebrews 3:13. Write it here:

Who I'm going to encourage:

We are protected from becoming hardened by the deceitfulness of sin by sticking with the flock and encouraging each other "while it is still called today" (Heb. 3:13, CSB).

Wait, let me check my braille watch. Yep, today is still called today. And, when we're done with this part of the study, it will still be called today. And until tomorrow comes, it will be called today.

That means you have the time and reason to encourage your Bible study buddies right now. Think of one of your buddies and one practical way you can encourage her today.

What I'm going to do to encourage her:

The writer of Hebrews quotes a psalm in the passage you just read. Read Hebrews 3:7-19 again, locate the included psalm, and write the reference— Hebrews 3:_____

Now cross-reference these verses.
Where is this section included in Psalms?

CROSS-REFERENCING HOW-TO

To cross-reference a verse or portion of a verse means to find other Scripture passages that are the same or similar. Many Bibles indicate cross-referenced verses in the footnotes or margins of the page. Also if part of a passage is a direct quote from another passage that will usually be indicated with all caps or bold. If your Bible doesn't tell you exactly where to find the quoted verse, you can find it by doing a Google or online search. Just remember to put quotation marks around the searchable phrase or verse. In this instance, you would search, "Today if you hear His voice, do not harden your hearts as when they provoked Me" (Heb. 3:8, NASB).

In case you missed it, the quoted portion is found in Hebrews 3:7b-11, and it comes from Psalm 95:7b-11. But the cool thing is how Psalm 95:7 starts:

... he is our God and we are the people of his pasture,
the flock under his care.
PSALM 95:7, NIV

It's a reminder that we are sheep. We are followers. We are vulnerable. We need to stay close to the Shepherd and in the flock. We need to stick together and encourage each other so we aren't deceived by sin's lie that says we can do it all, be what we want, and we don't need a Shepherd.

As you continue to study this verse this week, remember it is rooted in the understanding that sheep are under the shepherd's authority. When they submit, they get to lie down in green pastures and linger beside still waters.

We want all the green pastures and still waters God wants to give us, don't we?

Yes ma'am! See you tomorrow!

DAY 3

Hey there, my sister! Let's do a quick review as we start today. We've talked about how being safe with our Shepherd brings us rest. We've talked about how being under our Shepherd's authority brings us rest. And, now, we are going to get real practical about what kind of rest we're talking about.

I've already got my coffee—I hope you've got yours! Let's continue pulling apart Psalm 23:2. So far, we've played with the verbs in this verse and studied the pronouns. Now, let's talk about the nouns found in verse 2— the pastures and the waters.

IN GREEN PASTURES

Notice that there is an adjective describing the pasture. Never overlook any word in Scripture. The adjectives matter! What is it?

Look in your concordance, or do a search on your favorite online resource for *green pastures* or *pastures*. It may help to look at different Bible versions. Jot down a list of verses where these words show up. I've included some starters for you.

Jeremiah 23:10 • Ezekiel 34:14 • Joel 2:22 • _____

_____ • _____ • _____

After reading a variety of verses describing pastures, what do you think green pastures may represent?

Why do they exist? What is their purpose?

Green pastures are living and bring life. For sheep, they are a place of rest and a source of nourishment.

TWO KINDS OF GREEN PASTURES

Today, we'll look at two forms of green pastures: practices and pleasures. We need both.

Let's start with the green pasture pleasures. (Because it's just plain fun!)

Green pasture pleasures are the experiences, places, or activities that make you feel most alive. They relax or refresh you. They nourish your soul.

> Listening to a great audio book written by a dead author while I nibble on dark chocolate and smell a warm vanilla candle is a green pasture pleasure for me. So is riding our bicycle built for two and exploring antique stores. What are some of your green pasture pleasures? Be specific.

> My Green Pasture Pleasures:

> Have you enjoyed these pleasures lately? What happens to your attitude and your overall outlook on life when you go too long without green pasture pleasure?

We aren't as aware of our needs as God is. We don't recognize the signals that tell us we need to lie down in green pastures. But we have them. Some of my signals are impatience, a lack of joy, being forgetful and quick to cry—an overall Eeyore! When those things start to show up in my life, I know I need a green pasture. Put down your pen, or take your cute polished nails off your keyboard for just a minute and consider: Do you recognize the signals telling you it's time for a green pasture pleasure?

If so, list them below under Sheep Signals. If you aren't sure of your personal signals, ask God to reveal them to you. You can also ask a trusted friend or your husband—believe me, they will know!

My Sheep Signals:

It helps to identify our sheep signals. The Shepherd may use those to get our attention and turn our eyes toward Him so we will respond to His leading and follow Him.

We're all wired differently, so we'll have different green pasture *pleasure* interests and needs. But we all have in common the need for daily green pasture *practices*.

Green pasture practices have a lot in common with oxygen masks. Let me explain.

Every time I fly, I hear the same safety briefings. Some flight attendants announce them with perfect diction. Some take one big breath and cram the whole thing into a sixty second monosyllabic slur. And some drone on so long it makes me wish for a power outage that would initiate an emergency exit from the plane. I need to get out of there!

However, no matter the style or script, one thing the flight attendant always instructs the passengers to do is "put on your mask first before assisting the passenger next to you."

The spiel goes something like this: *If there is a sudden change in pressure, oxygen masks will drop from the compartment above you. Pull the mask toward you, place the yellow cup over your nose and mouth, securing the strap. If you are traveling with a child or someone who needs assistance, put on your mask first before securing theirs.*

Why does every flight attendant give this same instructions? Because if you try to help someone else get his or her mask on while you are gasping for air and turning blue, you quickly go from asset to liability.

You need to pay attention to your needs so you will be equipped to meet the needs of others. Your Shepherd wants to lead you to green pastures not just to bless and minister to you but so He can bless others and minister to others through you.

Just like you need oxygen every day, you need some green pasture visits every day. And, just as oxygen isn't optional, green pasture practices aren't optional either—you need them to breathe.

So what are green pasture practices?

These are the things you do daily to mitigate sheep signals showing up. These are the daily choices you make to take care of yourself, just as your Good Shepherd would want you to be cared for.

Green pasture practices fall into two basic categories.

1. YOUR BODY

Ask yourself the following:

- Do I get enough rest?

- Do I have a healthy diet?

- Do I exercise properly and frequently enough?

- Do my health habits prepare my body to help me do what I need and want to do?

- What are some better choices I can make concerning care for my body—i.e. rest, food, or exercise?

Girl, right now my treadmill has a layer of dust covering it. So do not hear for one single second that I am preaching a "get off the couch and be a workout queen who eats only organic every day" kind of message here! I am preaching grace, grace—grace only! I can't do this without God's grace because I personally am on-again, off-again with these kind of green pasture practices. (I am currently in an off-again spell that makes writing this pretty convicting. *Grimace.*)

I am constantly learning that the only way to care for my body as my Shepherd would want me to is to fall hard on His grace and follow Him to these green pastures. I've learned the hard way how run down and worn out I get when I don't. Here are two verses that remind me that God and His grace are at work in me: Philippians 1:6; 2:13. If this is hard for you, too, tell a Bible study buddy. I guarantee you are not alone. You can both lean on grace and each other—together we are stronger.

2. YOUR SOUL

Ask yourself the following:

- Is my soul fed everyday?

- Do I engage in activities that minister to my soul?

- Do I maintain spiritual habits that connect me to God and others?

- What are some better choices I can make that will feed and minister to my soul and connect me to God and others?

If we've been friends for long, you may know how significant that old hymn "It Is Well With My Soul" is to me. It was the very first song I played on the piano by ear after losing my sight as a 15-year-old girl. The truth is that even when it isn't well with our circumstances, it can be well with our souls. **Jesus ultimately makes it well with our soul.** *Thank You, Lord.*

He gives us opportunity to follow Him into green pastures every day, to keep it well with our souls. In other words, there are some things we can do so that it stays well with our souls. Reading Scripture, getting alone with God, and connecting with other Christ followers feed our souls, to name just a few practices. Experiencing some of those green pasture pleasures you listed earlier every now and then will minister to your soul too. Really pray about this, my sister. Your Shepherd wants you to follow Him into these green pasture practices. Through His grace He will give what you need to take care of your soul.

The flight attendant always precedes his or her oxygen mask monologue with, "In the unlikely event of an emergency ... " But here's the thing. You know as well as I do that emergencies aren't unlikely at all. They seem to happen quite often. Granted, there's a variance in how dire each emergency is. But we are going to have them. Inevitably we are going to be called on to put on someone's mask when we least expect it.

If we begin each day with the habit of putting on our masks first, we will be more equipped to fasten on others' masks when they need it most.

That means we need to develop green pasture practices that are customized for us. Don't try to copy your Bible study buddy's green pasture practices, find what works for you. You can do this, sister! Through God's grace, you can do whatever He leads you to do.

What are the green pasture practices you plan to start or restart?

Green pasture practices are choices we make, like choosing to reach up and pull down an oxygen mask. But sometimes we aren't tuned in. So stay close to the Shepherd; listen to His voice. Sometimes He uses your sheep signals as His gentle nudge to follow Him to a green pasture.

Are there some areas in your life where you aren't acknowledging your sheep signals? Do you need God to make you lie down in green pastures? If so, how would your life be different if you spent some time in green pastures?

If you want to be ambitious, search in a lexicon for the Hebrew word for *makes*. After some study, describe how the original Hebrew deepens, changes, or personalizes your understanding of the concept *makes* as found in Psalm 23:2. (I'll explain this to you when you watch the video this week.)

Girl, maybe this day is your day to respond to your sheep signals and follow your Shepherd to a green pasture. Do it, sister. You deserve it, and He is worthy of our surrender.

That was time well spent, wasn't it? Thanks for being honest with me about all this. I'm going to go dust off my treadmill and practice what I preach!

Lord, thank You for making us safe in You. We surrender to Your authority as our Shepherd, and we will follow You. Make us aware of our sheep signals, and make us lie down today in a green pasture.

Lord, lead us and we will follow. Amen.

DAY 4

No hot coffee for me today! I think we need something frosty because we're heading to the water. Put on your flip flops, and let's finish up verse 2 of Psalm 23!

HE LEADS ME BESIDE THE STILL WATERS

Since this feels like grammar week, we're going to keep at it. Find the adjective, or descriptor, that shows up before the word *waters* in Psalm 23:2. Now, pull out a dictionary, or go online to a thesaurus and jot down words that are opposite of and similar to *still*. (If you're a grammar geek, you are in heaven about now, right?)

Antonyms for *still*:

Synonyms for *still*:

Review the antonyms and synonyms you listed. What's your reaction to each group of words? Are the antonyms troubling? Are the synonyms encouraging?

The antonyms make me feel:

The synonyms make me feel:

Girl, I love words like *still, quiet, unmoving,* and *calm.* They are like windows in my soul that let in the fresh breeze and sunshine. They just make me relax or make me *want to* anyway! This is the description of the waters our Shepherd leads us to—*hmmm.*

The reason still waters are such a big deal to sheep is because they won't drink if the water is turbid or swift. They won't stick their little snouts into the stream. They know intuitively that they need still water. Still is calm. We need still waters too.

> Look in your concordance or do a word search on your favorite online Bible resource for Scriptures containing words such as *still* or *calm.* Next to each reference write the result of stillness or calmness. I listed some Scripture starters in case you need them.

STILL/CALM SCRIPTURE	RESULT OF *STILLNESS* AND *CALM*
Psalm 46:10	
Psalm 65:7	
Psalm 107:29	
Psalm 131:2	
Proverbs 14:30	
Mark 4:39	

Ah! When you read what you wrote in the results column, don't you just want all of that? I sure do! Scripture shows us over and over that when God calms and stills anything—storms or people—the result is rest, peace, a clearer understanding of who God is, and even health to our bodies.

BE STILL AND KNOW

Here's a question based on one of those Scriptures (Ps. 46:10).

What if you got still? How might it change what you know?

I don't mean still like striking a wax museum pose. And I don't mean getting still like shirking responsibility and quitting your job just to sit on the couch. I mean getting still in your soul, in your spirit. Creating a place in your soul to be quiet and know He is God, the sovereign God.

What if you really could *be still and know He is God*?

My friend, you can and you need to. I sure did and still do.

During a hard bout of depression a few years ago, I got really still. Two certainties surfaced: God is God. I am not, and I'm not supposed to be. Neither are you.

He is God over our problems and God over our pain. He is bigger than any mountain we face and stronger than any power we possess.

When I got still and learned in my deepest part of me that He is God, it freed me up from trying to fix and do. It let me just be me. Just be. It was another lesson from my Shepherd assuring me that it's OK to be a sheep. I am safe with Him.

I'll show you what I mean. Since we're friends now, you might as well read my journal from that time.

September 3, 2010

It's almost time for Connor to get home from school. I have just rested for an hour. I don't even know why. I don't even feel tired. But I feel overwhelmed by the vacuum I am living in at the moment. I lay there and asked the Lord, *what should I do?* I don't know what else to do. I am totally powerless, paralyzed, and overwhelmed. I know He just impressed me—I know I heard His voice echo in my heart. He said, *you should not do, you should be. Be still, and know that I am God.* Just be. I guess resting is being. I guess walking through this season with open hands to receive is just being, not doing. As I walk through this valley, I can be still. The Scripture doesn't tell me to be a fixer and know He is God. It doesn't tell me that I should do something so I will know He is God. He is reassuring me that I should simply be still—be—not run, fix, and do. I won't focus on doing; I will focus on being. *Even when I do have things I need to do, Lord, help me still to just be. Be still in You, rest in You, and know You are God. You are in charge. I can just be, and You will do all the doing that needs to be done in and through me. Thank You, Lord.*

So my friend, perhaps today you just need to take a deep breath and be still so you know that you are not God—He is. And He wants to meet you in your stress or sorrow. So slow down. In fact, stop. Stop trying to do and just be. Be still. Follow your Shepherd where He leads. Don't be so determined to follow your own plan. Quit striving to be the leader.

Take some time and be still by the water with your Shepherd. Take a walk with Him. Sit quietly with Him at your table or in your favorite chair. Let the windows in your soul open wide so the fresh breeze of His life can blow in, calm you, and give you rest. Quiet your world, quiet your heart, and just be with Him.

Yes, sister, I mean right now. You can come right back to finishing our study time together.

OK, now, let's continue to reflect on Psalm 46:10.

How does your life look on a daily basis as it relates to this verse? Would either of the following be true for you?

"Be a fixer, and know He is God."

Or maybe, "Be in control, and know he is God." OK, it's your turn. Fill in the blank that is true for where you are right now:

Be _____, and know He is God.

Write out a prayer to your Shepherd, or journal your thoughts about how you are currently living out this verse. Your words might reflect thankfulness because you're experiencing this peace. Or you might write a desperate request, asking God to help you be still so you will know that you are not God and He is. Ask Him to teach you more about this concept of being still in your soul. He will.

THE SHEPHERD LEADS, THE SHEEP FOLLOW

I'm so grateful that He's got us. He's in control. He gives us rest, and we're safe with our Shepherd. Now, let's identify one final part of speech for grammar week!

What is the verb that goes with still waters? What does your Shepherd do?

God leads you beside those still waters. He doesn't send you beside the still waters. He doesn't drag you to the still waters. He doesn't throw you in the deep end of the still waters so you can learn to swim. He *leads* you.

Journal your thoughts about why He leads you to still waters instead of just giving you a map and expecting you to find your own way. What does leading suggest about God's character and care for you?

For sheep, still waters are the source to quench their thirst. What are or where are the still waters in your life? What helps you know that He is God? What brings you peace, clarity, and health?

If you haven't been by still waters as much as you need to, what is one choice you can make to help you get there more often?

Can you think of ways God leads you to still waters?

I would have never thought in a million years that when I was in the thick of depression I was also being led beside still waters. God used that dry time in my life as still waters in disguise—a time to quench a deeper thirst within me. It was one I didn't even know I had until the need was met. He lovingly led me beside still waters. He showed me I could trust Him to be my Shepherd, and I could just be a sheep. I could just follow and rest in Him.

Have you had any situations in your life that were still waters in disguise? If so, what did you learn about your Shepherd? What did you learn about yourself?

For sheep to get what they need from their shepherd, they must be willing to obey when he makes them lie down in green pastures. And they must be willing to follow when he leads them to the still waters. They must put themselves under the shepherd's authority. If they stubbornly dig their little hooves into the pasture or ignore the shepherd's guidance, they won't be where they need to be in order to get what they need.

Your soul has needs too. Rest. Nourishment. Peace. Companionship. Refreshment. Are you positioned to receive what your soul needs most? Don't walk away today until you get this settled between you and your Shepherd. This matters because you matter, my sweet sister.

After studying this beautiful verse, don't you want to just take a deep breath and lean into your Shepherd? Don't you just want to stay in that position through every moment of every day? Me too, sister.

DAY 5

GREEN PASTURE DAY: A DAY TO REST AND DIGEST

He makes me to lie down in green pastures;

He leads me beside the still waters.

PSALM 23:2

This is your day to do whatever helps you really digest what you've learned this week. It's also a chance for you just to rest, pray, journal, draw, worship, or ponder. I've included some practical things this week to help give legs to what we've learned. But don't feel pressure to respond. Just do what is helpful.

Here are some things to consider as you rest and digest:

My Green Pasture Practice plan:

My Green Pasture pleasure bucket list:

Still waters I want to include in my life:

Scriptures I want to remember from this week:

Quotes I liked from this week:

Thank You, Lord, for the green pastures and still waters. Lead me to them, and I will follow.

Be a Hebrews 3:13 girl! Share on Facebook® something from this week that encouraged you so it can encourage others. If you're on Instagram®, take a picture of yourself in a green pasture practice or pleasure and share it to encourage your Bible study buddies. (Tag me @JennRothschild so I will know, please!) Or text a friend a Scripture to give her the boost she needs.

To help you meditate on the truths you've experienced in this verse, listen to the songs I've included in my *Psalm 23* playlist. (You'll find the playlist at JenniferRothschild.com/Psalm23.)

GROUP SESSION 3

BEFORE THE VIDEO

Welcome and Prayer

VIDEO NOTES

Our Shepherd, who supplies all our needs, knows that we need _____.

Four Things Sheep Require to Rest

1. Sheep must be free from _____.

2. Sheep must be free from _____.

3. Sheep must be free from _____.

4. Sheep must be free from _____.[1]

Verbs in Psalm 23:2

1. He _____ us lie down.

- "He makes me lie down" can also be interpreted as "He _____ me down."

- We don't get what we need because there is so much that we _____.

- If you don't pause, you don't receive _____.

- Psalm 23:2 is about God's _____ and our _____ to His authority.

2. He _____ us.

- We don't need to look for _____ _____. We only need to look to the Shepherd, and He _____ us to the still waters.

When We Position Ourselves Under Our Shepherd's Authority:

R   He _____ our fear.

E   He _____ our friction.

S   He _____ our distractions.

T   "_____ and see that the LORD is good" (Psalm 34:8).

CONVERSATION GUIDE
Video 3

DAY 1: In what situations do you find it difficult to rest?
What is your favorite "safe" Scripture? Why?
Does being safe with the Shepherd mean you'll never face difficulty? If not, what does it mean?

DAY 2: Do you spend more time looking for green pastures than you do looking to your Shepherd? Explain.
What is the link between our surrender to God and the rest we receive from God?
How does sticking with the flock keep us from being deceived?

DAY 3: What are some of your Green Pasture Pleasures and Green Pasture Practices?

DAY 4: How difficult is it for you to be still? Explain.
What is one intentional choice you need to make to help you get to those still waters more often?

DAY 5: Share some of the highlights from your Green Pasture Day.
What is one significant truth you take away from this week of study?

> Need to be reminded of what you just heard? Get my written summary of this video teaching at jenniferrothschild.com/psalm23.

YOUR SHEPHERD GUIDES YOUR PATH

He restores my soul; He leads
me in the paths of righteousness
for His name's sake.

PSALM 23:3

DAY 1

He restores my soul; He leads me in the paths
of righteousness for His name's sake.

PSALM 23:3

Is it just me, or can you believe the depth and the richness of this tiny psalm? So much is packed into it! Are you ready for verse 3? Have a seat, and let's start with prayer.

Oh Lord, our Shepherd, lead us into truth this week as we study Your beautiful Word. Quiet our hearts, clear our minds, and draw us to Yourself. Amen.

HE RESTORES

I just brewed some tea, and it's sitting here in an old silver teapot waiting for us to start. Girl, I love this piece. She is from the late 1800s, and she's not just full of the most fragrant black tea. She's full of attitude—fancy, fluted, Victorian elegance, pomp, and British attitude! Besides that, Her Royal Highness keeps my tea hot for hours. I decided I'd start today with some proper tea because using this teapot helps me connect with this verse. You'll see why in a minute.

If you haven't turned there yet, go to Psalm 23:3 in your Bible, and read it aloud. It features four of the most appealing, beautiful, promising words in Scripture—"He restores my soul."

Ahh, what woman doesn't love that—what woman doesn't need that? Let's start this week of study learning and living those words—"He restores my soul."

Now, even though we've already studied the first two verses of this psalm, jot down again who wrote it:

I know you know it's David, but it's important to always remember our context because the context helps us understand the text.

Throughout this psalm, David compares himself to a what?

What do the personal pronouns that David uses remind us about the relationship between him and the Lord, and between us and our Shepherd? (Review verse 1 again, for reference.)

David is writing this out of the knowledge that He belongs to His Shepherd. We need to read it the same way. Ancient and modern shepherds alike don't just walk up on a hill, notice some sheep, and start caring for them.

Shepherds choose and purchase their sheep. They own them. The sheep are the possession of the shepherd.

That means, we can't go any farther without a gut honest question.

Do you belong to the Shepherd?

In other words, have you responded to the call of Christ, turned from your sin, and turned toward Him? Is Jesus your Savior and Lord?

Girl, none of this will make a bit of sense if you don't know Jesus. Knowing *about* Him isn't the same as knowing Him. Before we go to the next paragraph, respond honestly here. If you're not sure, call a Bible study buddy or a friend who walks with Christ, and ask her to help you with this. You don't even need to worry about what to say, just read her this last paragraph!

If you do belong to the Shepherd, if you have been born again in Christ, on the following page, jot down how and when that happened. And then thank Him for making you His own.

The Lord became my Shepherd on or when ...

Thank You, Lord, for becoming my Shepherd and making me ...

OK, now back to explaining the connection between the teapot and today's verse. The reason I'm pouring tea from this teapot is because she's been restored. In fact, Her Royal Highness was rescued and restored thanks to my mom's ability to see beyond the grunge that hid the teapot's beauty.

Mom spotted her in a thrift store—tarnished, dusty, and black from years of neglect. But my mom saw right through the grime. My mom knew her value. So, she purchased her and used a whole tub of silver polish to make her shine. Mom probably got tendinitis in the process of cleaning off all the gunk. But the result is "Wow!" My mom restored the teapot; she brought her back to her original luster.

But, she had to rescue her first.

God rescued us too. Read Ephesians 2:12-13, and answer the following.

My condition before God rescued me (Weave Ephesians 2:12 into your answer.):
I was ...

My condition after God rescued me (Weave Ephesians 2:13 into your answer.):
I am ...

Before our Shepherd rescued us and brought us to Himself, we were separated from Him, lost, excluded, and without hope. Bleak picture, isn't it? But after He drew us to

Himself and purchased us with His precious blood, He became our peace. We are His, brought near by the blood of Christ.

So when David says his Shepherd restores his soul, he's talking restoration not rescue.

Our Shepherd rescued our souls from sin. He restores our souls when we stray.

When our Shepherd restores our souls, He is bringing us back from our ignorance, errors, and wanderings.

Go to your concordance or favorite online study resource and do a word search for *restore*. Jot down the verses you find, and note what each verse says about *restoration*. I've given you some Scripture starters to get you headed in the right direction.

SCRIPTURE	NOTES ON *RESTORATION*
Deuteronomy 30:1-3	
Psalm 80:3	
Jeremiah 30:17	
Jeremiah 33:7	
Galatians 6:1	

Use the verses in the list to craft a biblical definition of *restore*. Think about what is required to be restored. Think about what God restores us to.

My biblical definition of *restore:*

The original Hebrew for *restore* in Psalm 23:3 means *to bring back* or *return.*[1]

No one restores silver or furniture if it has no value. No one wastes the energy or work to restore something that has no potential. What does that say about the reason God chooses to restore you?

Do you believe you are that valuable to your Shepherd? I think this question requires a Scripture revisit!

Read Psalm 119:176 and Matthew 18:12-13. What do both of those passages have in common?

What do they say about your value to the Shepherd?

Every sheep matters to the Shepherd.

He parties big-time when one is restored. He seeks the ones who stray so they can be returned to Him and to the flock.

That's you, sister! That's me. We are that valuable to God. Amazing, isn't it?

> Now put down your pen a minute and just read Psalm 103:13-14. It describes how your Shepherd responds to you when you blow it, stray, and need restoration once again. Fill in the spaces below to help focus your thoughts.
>
> God shows me ...
>
>
>
> God knows I am ...

Now, here's the question. Do you admit and accept that God knows your weakness, that He knows you are about as strong and sturdy as dust? Do you accept the compassion God shows you?

Sister, we are sheep. It's OK to be a sheep. We honor and love our Shepherd by receiving His compassion and pressing into His restoration. Before you move on, spend some time with your Shepherd. Thank Him. Enjoy His company. Receive what you need from Him right now.

> *Oh Lord, my Shepherd,*
>
>
>
>
>
> *Amen.*

Our Shepherd shows compassion to us because He knows we're weak, fragile creatures. And He doesn't just bring us back from our wanderings, He gives us back what our wanderings have taken from us.

Here's the thing, sister. When we stray from our Shepherd, in whom we lack nothing, we will lack many things. Emotionally, we may start to crumble. Mentally, we may become deceived. Our spirits may become depleted. In other words, our souls take a hit.

That's why God restores your soul. He brings restoration to your whole person.

MY SOUL

So what exactly is a soul? How would you define it?

The Hebrew word for soul is *nephesh* and it can be translated *soul, life, heart,* or *mind.*[2]

We find this word in other Scripture passages, including Genesis 2:7. Read the verse and describe what happened when God breathed into the man He shaped from dust. What did the man become?

Depending on your Bible version, you may find he became a living creature, living being, or living soul.

Nephesh is the God-breathed you, the essence of you, the part of you that will outlive your body. It's the core of you that makes you you—your mind, heart, will, and spirit! It's the you that your Shepherd restores.

So, how's your *nephesh*? I bet nobody has asked you that in a while! Does your *nephesh* need to be restored? Spend some time with your Shepherd and pray through and/or journal the following:

What broken places in my heart need restoration?

What tattered emotions need to be returned to health?

What wandering or wrong thoughts need to be brought back to truth?

What waywardness in my will needs a 180° change of direction?

What spiritually empty places need to be filled up again?

When God restores our souls, it is well with our souls.

Let's clarify something important about this verse. Does it say that *you* restore your soul or that *God* restores your soul?

Bingo! It ain't up to us, sister! It's all about the Shepherd.

Just as my teapot couldn't rescue herself, she can't restore herself either. As she gets tarnished, she doesn't clean herself up. I do it for her.

Just as a sheep can't buy her way into a flock, she can't find her way back to the flock when she wanders either. The shepherd is the one who buys the sheep, and the shepherd is the one who brings back the sheep.

Just like God rescued your soul, He is the One who restores your soul—over and over, every time you need it.

God does the work of restoration and here's how He does it.

Read Psalm 19:7 and Ephesians 5:26. How does God do that for you?

What you are doing right now by spending time in God's Word—the Law of the Lord, His precepts—is part of your soul's constant cleansing and restoration.

That's why we stay in His Word during the daily walk of our lives. Being in His Word won't keep all the dirt and dings of this world away from you, but being in His Word will keep all the dirt and dings of this world from tarnishing your beauty and weakening your stability. His living and active Word restores you every single day.

It seems to me that Psalm 23:2 and the first part of verse 3 can be read as one beautiful cause and effect thought: "He makes me to lie down in green pastures; He leads me beside the still waters; He restores my soul." Meaning, the result of all that obeying, following, resting, and receiving is soul restoration.

Ah, what a beautiful way to live.

I guess it's about time we wind it up. But before we go, I want to share with you how I meditate on what I'm learning from the Lord. I hope this will be useful for you as we continue to learn together through our study of Psalm 23.

Here are five Rs to contemplate as you go through the rest of your day. Write them on a sticky note, and use them to study your heart and to keep learning this truth about restoration:

1. REVIEW—Is it well with my soul? Are my mind, will, emotions, and spirit healthy and at peace? Do I need restoration?

2. REPENT—Am I hurting my own soul by my own choices? Have I willingly strayed from my Shepherd and my identity in Him? Is there an about-face I need in my attitude or actions?

3. RETURN—Am I ready to be brought back so it will be well with my soul again?

4. RESTORE—Do I need and want my Shepherd to restore my soul?

5. RECEIVE—Am I willing to humbly receive all my Shepherd wants to give me?

Alrighty, sister—see you tomorrow!

DAY 2

Hey there! I wonder where you're studying Psalm 23 today? I'm actually sitting out on the deck because it's beautiful outside. The breeze is cool, and the sun is warm. I've just been pondering this verse and praying through it. So, I thought we would do it together as we start. Yesterday, we talked about how our Shepherd restores our souls. Today, we'll explore how He guides us.

Take a moment and slowly read each word from this phrase of the verse. Say aloud and meditate on each word, one at a time. You may want to journal your thoughts. And, sister, don't rush. Spend time meditating on God's Word. Let it restore and refresh your soul.

... HE GUIDES ME IN THE PATHS OF RIGHTEOUSNESS ...
PSALM 23:3, NASB

As you meditate on the verse, consider these questions:

HE—Who is He? Who is He to you?

HE GUIDES—What does it mean to guide? Why is He qualified to guide you? Where has He guided you in the past?

HE GUIDES ME—Did you notice another "He and me" phrase here? What images come to mind when you think of a one-on-one guide? What does that say about your Shepherd and His relationship to you?

IN THE PATHS—What is the purpose of a path? What makes a path? What path are you on? How has God guided you?

OF RIGHTEOUSNESS—What does righteousness mean? What makes a path righteous?

I hope those prompts give you some idea of how to pull each word out of a verse and examine it as a precious gem. (We'll look at *for His name's sake* later.)

Now put all the words back together just as a master jeweler would set each beautiful diamond in a stunning cluster—each gem enhancing the beauty of the others. Take a look at the phrase again as it shines so beautifully. Now change the pronoun from *He* to *You*, and personalize this phrase into a prayer to your Shepherd. Draw from your meditation time to continue to personalize the verse into a prayer.

Dear Lord,

_____ restore my soul; _____ guide me in the paths of righteousness for _____ name's sake (NASB).

Amen.

When you personalize that Scripture, it's like moving from observing a beautiful diamond cluster ring to receiving it as a gift and placing it on your finger. Oh girl, it looks good on you!

Now, after meditating on and praying through that whole phrase, let's study it together.

Clearly you know the *He* is God, our Shepherd. So look at what He does. He guides. Do a word search for *guide* in your concordance or on your favorite online resource. Find Scriptures that describe God's guidance. (Expand your search by looking for other phrases that express the concept of guidance, such as *show the way* or *lead*.)

Next to each verse you find, describe how God guides you, where He guides you, or what happens without His guidance. Use "I" statements.

SCRIPTURE	HOW GOD GUIDES ME
Psalm 5:8	
Psalm 25:4-5,9	
Psalm 31:3	
Psalm 86:11	
Proverbs 11:14	

Based on the Scriptures I found, it's pretty obvious that I need guidance. Without it I can stray or stumble. And thankfully, God is so willing to teach me the way and instruct me where I should go. Let's make this practical.

Close your eyes.

Well, duh. I guess you can't close your eyes and keep reading. I can because my computer talks! Ha! So after you read this, close your eyes. When you do, pay attention to what you see or don't see. Imagine you had to walk from where you are to your refrigerator with your eyes closed. How would you feel? If you're brave, try it. I'll wait.

It probably wasn't easy, was it? And it may have been dangerous or comical. The truth is, when you can't see, life is a whole lot easier if you have a guide—someone to lead you, show you the way, and teach you where to step so you end up in the right place.

That's why your Shepherd guides you—so you end up on the right path.

Being blind, I need a guide—someone I can trust and hold on to so I can get to the right place. Your vision may be 20/20 (or close), but you need a guide too. You have to do what I do—trust and hold on to your Shepherd so you find and stay on the right path.

Do you trust Him? Are you willing to follow? Even when the path gets bumpy, difficult, or confusing?

Let's be honest with each other. As I type those questions, everything inside me is saying *Yes!* And that truly is my heart's desire and intention. But, I don't want to settle for just desire and good intention. I want the liberty and power that comes from really, really, really trusting Him and living like it. To answer honestly, if I trust Him, I have to ask bluntly, *Who do I follow? What guides me?*

Who or what I follow is who or what I trust most. It's not what I say, it's what I do that proves who or what I trust.

So, I studied my heart and made two lists of all the things I can potentially follow—what potentially guides me. Then I created another list to consider which guide I find the most trustworthy.

Pause and ask God's Spirit to lead you into truth right here, right now. Circle below what applies to you, or add your own items to the lists.

WHAT GUIDES ME?	WHAT DO I TRUST MOST?
My Emotions	My Emotions
My History	My History
My Habits	My Habits
My Personality	My Personality
My Will	My Will
My Experience	My Experience
My Dysfunction	My Dysfunction
My Family Dynamics	My Family Dynamics
My Opinion	My Opinion
My Pastor	My Pastor
God's Grace	God's Grace
God's Word	God's Word
God's Spirit	God's Spirit
Other:	Other:

You may have circled lots of things, and that's OK. Many things I listed are good guides—my pastor, my opinions, my experience, and so forth. All of those have merit. But none are worthy of being my only and ultimate guide. If I only follow my opinion, I could be wrong. If I trust my experience exclusively, it could be incomplete. If I blindly follow my pastor, he could accidentally mislead because he is human. You get the idea.

Look at what you circled and take some time to pray about this.

Lord, please be our guide. We want to trust You more than our experiences, feelings, habits, or anyone and anything else in our lives. It is You, Your Word, and Your Spirit that we want to follow. Thank You for leading and guiding us, Lord. Amen.

OK, I'm just being real here, and I hope you are too.

If we really trust the Lord, He will be our ultimate guide in all things, right?

How does that happen in an everyday, real world sort of way?

You know the answer. The way He guides us is the same way He restores our souls. Remember what that is?

Check out the following verses to confirm the way God leads us, and jot down how each verse shows how practical His guidance is.

Psalm 119:24—God's Word is my ...

Psalm 119:105—God's Word is my ...

Psalm 119:130—God's Word is my …

Girl, just as the shepherd's voice leads the sheep, our Shepherd's voice, through His Word, guides us.

We are like sheep, and sheep have no GPS! They need a guide and so do we. God's Word is our guide. It directs our steps. It illuminates our path. It makes us wise and gives us insight. When we trust our Shepherd to guide us, we trust His Word to be our GPS.

Well, sister, my heart is full, and I still have lots to think and pray about. Let's call it a day and hang out again tomorrow. We'll end with this passage from The Message. Eugene Peterson paraphrased the beginning of Psalm 119 like this:

> You're blessed when you stay on course,
> walking steadily on the road revealed by GOD.
> You're blessed when you follow his directions,
> doing your best to find him.
> That's right—you don't go off on your own;
> you walk straight along the road he set.
> You, GOD, prescribed the right way to live;
> now you expect us to live it.
> Oh, that my steps might be steady,
> keeping to the course you set;
> Then I'd never have any regrets
> in comparing my life with your counsel.
> I thank you for speaking straight from your heart;
> I learn the pattern of your righteous ways.
> I'm going to do what you tell me to do;
> don't ever walk off and leave me.
> **PSALM 119:1-8, THE MESSAGE**

And to that I say, thank You, Lord!

DAY 3

He restores. He guides. That's what we've talked about so far this week. Now, how do we know that where we are is the right path? Well, pour your coffee or tea or grab your water bottle, and let's find out.

PATHS OF RIGHTEOUSNESS

Our Shepherd guides us in paths of righteousness. Like any good shepherd, our Shepherd doesn't drive us—He leads us.

The Hebrew verb used in this verse for *guide* is in "the Hiphil form," which emphasizes causative action.[3] In other words, you could phrase it as, "He causes me to be led down paths of righteousness … " Your Shepherd is the One "causing" you to be guided in the paths of righteousness. What a relief! It's not you by yourself. It's not your own independent thinking and will. God's grace gets you on the path, and His grace keeps you on the path.

Your Shepherd causes you to be led down the paths He chooses for you. Now, I know this can get fuzzy because I was a little confused as I studied this. So think of it this way: Phil and I purchased our sweet, little dog, Lucy, in 2010. She is a fun, little diva dog whose grooming costs more than mine. When we walk, I guide her. I "cause" her to be led by me. How do I do that when she is an independent creature with a strong will? I attach a sparkly, blinged-up leash to her so we are connected. That way, she is assured to go on the right path. She may know the way, but without the leash, she may or may not go on the right path—it all depends on the new doggie smells along the way that may distract her. However, she is guaranteed to be on the right path when she is connected to me. And truly, the only time either of us even notice the leash is when she disobeys, gets distracted, or ignores my commands. I cause her to be led. She follows.

Now, in case you think I am comparing us to my diva dog Lucy (maybe that is a step up from sheep)—well, I guess I am! (Lucy is so cute and so are you!)

When we belong to our Shepherd, we are connected to Him. He has drawn us with "ropes of love" (Hos. 11:4, CSB), and He lovingly stays one step ahead of us to keep us on the right path. He causes us to be led by Him.

Girl, we don't have to know the path; we just need to know the Shepherd. When we stay connected to Him, when we trust and follow, we are led down the best path for us—the right path.

So let's find Scripture that affirms how He causes us to be guided in the right paths.

Use the Scripture starters below, and find other Scripture passages with the word *path* or *way*. Complete the sentence in the second column. I've finished one as an example.

SCRIPTURE	HE CAUSES ME TO BE LED BY ...
Psalm 16:11	REVEALING THE PATH OF LIFE TO ME.
Psalm 32:8	
Proverbs 2:8	
Proverbs 3:5-6	
Isaiah 30:21	

Did you notice the different ways God causes us to be guided? Your Shepherd's guidance is never strong-armed. He doesn't cause you to be guided by yanking and prodding, pushing you and pulling you along. Isn't it interesting how many verses show that He causes you to be led by His voice?

In the Holy Land, shepherds most often guide with their voices. Frequently a shepherd will sing, and his sheep know his voice. It's not uncommon for several shepherds and their flocks to be at a water source all at the same time. Often, flocks mingle. They will drink and then be made to lie down and rest while the shepherds catch up on all the latest shepherd gossip.

When a shepherd is finished catching up on the news and is ready to go, he calls his sheep or begins to sing. His sheep instinctively separate themselves from the other flocks. They will quickly stand, leave the snoozing flocks behind, and walk to their shepherd because they recognize His voice. I've heard that it is amazing to see.

If you'd like to see a video of sheep following their shepherd's voice, just do a search on YouTube for "sheep obey master's voice." You'll find real-life videos of sheep responding to their shepherd's voice.

Your Shepherd is always calling to you and for you. He leads you with His voice.

Do you hear His voice through His Word and His Spirit? When you do, you can have one of two responses.

Write the response each verse indicates:

1. John 10:27

2. Hebrews 3:15

A sheep can hear her shepherd's voice and follow him. Or she can just lie there with the other sheep, dig her little hoofs into the pasture, and harden her heart. Which best describes you?

Oh girl, hard-hearted sheep miss out. If I am walking with Lucy and she gets obstinate or distracted, there is tension. I feel it. She feels it. And it doesn't feel good. If we hear and follow, we will be on the path—the right path. If we harden our hearts when we hear His voice, we will feel nothing but tension. His voice always leads us to righteousness.

Find a dictionary definition of *righteous*, and write it below.

Chances are you found a definition that suggested something like "accepted moral standards" or "just behavior." The original Hebrew word for *righteous* used in Psalm 23 can also be translated as "rightness" or "straight." It's often used to describe fair weights and scales—precise, accurate, not unfairly weighted, right.[4]

But here's the way I like to think of righteousness: In the 1970s, tie-dyed teenagers started saying, "Right on." And I've noticed that those aging hippies are still saying it! (I may or may not be one of them who used that phrase while Sonny and Cher or Cat Stevens blared from my radio.) I love it because it means: *exactly correct, in agreement.*

In many ways, a path of righteousness is a right-on kind of walk. Meaning, it's correct, in agreement with God's Word. It's not wobbly or wayward or watered down or weird. It's just right—right on! Groovy, huh?

John Piper says, "A path of righteousness is a right path followed with the right attitude."[5] If you are following your Shepherd as He guides you down a right path, are you on it with the right attitude?

Honesty alert! Honesty alert! I must interrupt your regularly scheduled Bible study to tell you what just happened. I'm sitting out here on the deck looking over a beautiful, quiet lake. It is like God has led me beside the still waters—literally. I'm leaning back in a wicker rocker, wrapped in a blanket, with my computer on my lap pondering our paths of righteousness. It is peaceful. Here we are, me, my Shepherd, and you. I'm praying and studying and writing about our right paths. I hear cicadas and an occasional lap of water as the lake gently sways.

And then—I hear nothing except *ROAR! VAROOOOOOOOOOOOM! REVVING ROAR!*

The loudest, most obnoxious motor I have ever heard in my entire life. It sounds like the million man Harley-Davidson® convention just convened on the boat dock in front of me. Seriously, the engine on the offending boat must be at full throttle. It's so loud my deck is vibrating!

I write on a computer that talks to me, and I cannot hear one word. So I take my fingers off the keyboard and haughtily flick my hand, pointing at that noise and scolding out loud, "You idiot! Do you think you are the only one on this lake?" Yes, I'm yelling in a very unChristian sort of way at the loud boat that can't hear me while I'm writing a Bible study. (And thankfully, no one else could see me. If so, there goes the testimony.) Boy, did I wander away quickly from those still waters. I stumbled on that path of righteousness.

Plus, I had just written that question, "Are you on the right path with the right attitude?" *BAM!* Sister, I can't get away with anything! Ha!

Am I where I am supposed to be? Yep. Am I on the path God guided me to? Yep. Am I on this right path with the right attitude? Uh, clearly not.

The point is, I can be wrong even on the right path. That's why I need God's Word and Spirit to constantly guide me and keep my soul restored. I have a feeling I'm not the only one. *Grin.*

Now, back to our regularly scheduled Bible study. We can have wrong attitudes and actions on our right paths. But righteous paths can also feel wrong sometimes because they may be bumpy and hard. Sometimes the shepherd has to lead his sheep through tight places and rough terrain to get them where the pastures are better. Right paths may not always feel right, but where the Shepherd leads you is always right.

Girl, we don't control the path. All we control is our attitude and actions on the path. So if your path is a little rough, instead of questioning the path, trust the Guide.

When Phil and I are on long drives, (No, I am not driving.) he often uses the road signs on the highway to give him that umph he needs when he's tired of such a long road. It's those signs that remind him he's in the right place, going the right direction. And they encourage him to keep on trucking! We need those road signs too, sister.

> On the path below, write in some Scripture road signs—verses that encourage you to keep following your Shepherd and keep walking on that path of righteousness. Here are some Scriptures you can use for encouragement on your path: Acts 20:24; Romans 8:28; Philippians 2:13; 3:14.

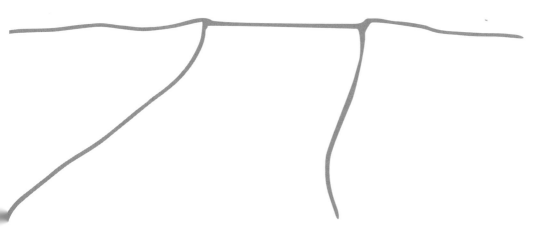

One last thought before we go.

Were you ever in a math class where the teacher worked out some magnificently complicated equation on the board? If you're like me, you sat in class, trembling with fear, hoping and praying the teacher wouldn't call on you to explain the work. As each step in solving the problem was demonstrated, you sat there dazed and confused with absolutely no idea what was happening on that chalkboard. But eventually, the equal sign was drawn; the answer followed it; and low and behold, it was right. It was exactly correct. You had no idea why it turned out right, you just knew it was right.

Your path may sometimes feel like that math problem. You may not understand all the twists and turns, but if you're following the Shepherd, you can trust that even the parts that don't make sense are right and will lead you to rightness. So don't get discouraged if your path is confusing. Just like the teacher held the chalk and was working out the equation, God is holding your heart, your life, and the map. He is working it all out—it's right on.

Stay in His Word, and you will stay in His will.

It's that simple, that profound.

But the path of the righteous is like the light of dawn,
that shines brighter and brighter until the full day.
PROVERBS 4:18, NASB

Thank You, Lord!

DAY 4

Well, here we are at the end of this verse. It is so rich, and I'm learning so much. Read Psalm 23:3 again, and ask the Lord your Shepherd to guide you into truth today.

The right path that God's Word guides us to and guide us on has a purpose. And believe it or not, the ultimate purpose has absolutely not one thing to do with us, our preferences, or our pleasures.

> What do the last four words of verse 3 say about the purpose of that righteous path?

FOR HIS NAME'S SAKE

Girl, the path God guides us to and guides us on is full of promise and potential. It has purpose, but the path isn't chosen for my sake. And it's not for your sake. It's for God's sake— for His name's sake.

> What do you think that means?

The more you read Scripture, the better you understand that God takes His name pretty seriously.

Using your concordance or favorite online resource, find some verses that show how God feels about His name. (You can use *my name* or *the name* to help you locate them in your search.)

Read each verse as a prayer of affirmation to the Lord. Linger a bit with each verse, and get a renewed sense of God's grandeur and otherness. I've provided a few verses and a place to phrase them into a prayer of worship below.

Exodus 20:3-5 • Isaiah 42:8 • Malachi 1:11 • Philippians 2:9

Amen.

God's name represents His character. God always acts according to His character and, ultimately, for His name's sake.

Even human shepherds lead their sheep for "their names' sake." They choose the paths for their sheep in order to protect their own reputations as good shepherds. The path a shepherd chooses reflects the shepherd's character—his management of his sheep, his integrity, his compassion, and his ability. The condition of the sheep is a reflection of the shepherd.

God's honor is at stake in the way He is leading your life. That's why what He is doing for you and in you is ultimately for His name's sake.

Let's confirm that thought through Scripture. Search through a concordance or online resource to find examples of what God does for His name's sake. Add what you find to my Scripture starters.

SCRIPTURE	WHAT GOD DOES FOR HIS NAME'S SAKE
Psalm 25:11	
Isaiah 48:9	
Jeremiah 14:7	
Ezekiel 20:9	

When psalmists and prophets appealed to God to act for His name's sake, they were pleading for God to act according to His character, not according to what they deserved.

God forgives us for His name's sake. He delays wrath for His name's sake. He leads us for His name's sake. God explained it through Ezekiel when He said:

> It is not for your sake, people of Israel, that I am going to
> do these things, but for the sake of my holy name.
> **EZEKIEL 36:22, NIV**

Here's the thing, sister, we all tend to live our life stories as if we are the main characters of our own lives. But girl, we aren't. God is.

He forgives us because He loves us, yes. He restores us because He values us, yes. But ultimately, it is not about us. What God does, He does for His name's sake. His actions are for His praise. The beautiful benefit, though, is that what brings Him glory brings us good.

> As you look back on your path, can you see how God has guided you for His name's sake? If so, how? What has brought Him glory along your path?

> The name of the Lord is holy and higher than any other name. So if He guides you down right paths for His name's sake, what does that suggest about the purpose of your path and your attitude on the path?

My friend, you may be on a path that is hard and bumpy. Although it's the right path, you sometimes wonder if it's wrong because it isn't easy. Hang in there! If the Shepherd is leading, you can absolutely know and trust that God is guiding you through this season for His glory, and the result will be your good.

> How does understanding this truth help you take the next step?

As we experience daily restoration from the Lord, we are guided by His Word and His Spirit down the exact path that is good for us and brings glory to Him. Don't you just love it? You, a lowly sheep, can bring glory to the Shepherd by simply trusting, following, and obeying.

You don't have to be on a big stage speaking to thousands to glorify God. You don't have to be on a mission field in the deepest jungle to bring Him glory. Sure, those actions and life circumstances can glorify Him, but the best way you bring God glory is through your humble trust and obedience in an everyday walk with Him. So sister, stay in His Word so you will live under His will.

We've had a good week, haven't we? I hope you are loving Psalm 23. But most of all, I hope you are falling more in love with the Shepherd of Psalm 23. Did you notice that this verse really isn't about our path, its about God's praise—it's for His name's sake!

Lord, we love You. In You we live and move and have our being (Acts 17:28). All things are from You, through You, and to You—to You be the glory forever (Rom. 11:36). It is all for Your name's sake. Amen!

DAY 5

GREEN PASTURE DAY: A DAY TO REST AND DIGEST

He restores my soul; He leads me in the paths
of righteousness for His name's sake.
PSALM 23:3

As you use this day to do whatever helps you really digest what you've learned this week, consider that Psalm 23:3 helps us understand a praise principle: we are restored and guided on right paths for our Shepherd's praise.

On your Green Pasture Day, as you rest, pray, journal, draw, worship, or ponder, here are some things to consider:

How I experienced the Shepherd's guidance this week:

How I see God working out His purpose in and through my life:

Scriptures I want to remember from this week:

Quotes I liked from this week:

Thank You, Lord, for restoring my soul and guiding me down right paths for Your name's sake.

To help you meditate on the truths you've experienced in this verse, you can listen to the songs I included in my *Psalm 23* playlist. (Find it at JenniferRothschild.com/Psalm23.)

GROUP SESSION 4

BEFORE THE VIDEO

Welcome and Prayer

VIDEO NOTES

"A path of righteousness is a right path followed with the _____ attitude."[5]

—John Piper

We all travel different paths; but we all have the same destination—_____

_____.

Three Things Our Paths Have in Common

1. We have the same on-ramp, which is _____.

   • Psalm 23:3 is referring to being _____ through grace.

   • *Being restored* means to literally "bring us _____."

   • Every time we _____, He rescues us.

   • God restores us to our true _____.

2. Our paths are for our _____.

   • We can be on the right path and it can feel _____.

RIGHT PATHS CAN FEEL WRONG BECAUSE

A. We are in the HOV lane. The path may be stressful and feel wrong. But if God put you on the path, it has _____.

B. We are stuck in traffic. Suddenly we can feel _____ and question our path.

   • We can feel like our path is suddenly _____.

C. We are on the shoulder. _____ life happens.

 • Be patient because your path is for your _____ .

3. The destination is _____ _____.

 • Whatever brings God glory will _____ us _____.

The condition of the sheep is a reflection of the shepherd's _____.

Where you are right now may _____ _____ but that doesn't mean it's _____ _____.

CONVERSATION GUIDE
Video 4

DAY 1: Do you belong to the Shepherd? Share your story of how you came to your faith relationship with Christ.
How has God restored your soul after a situation or season of rebellion?

DAY 2: How have you experienced the Shepherd's guidance in the past?
What are some things or people you look to for guidance instead of the Shepherd? Why do we so easily turn to these guides?
What situation are you presently facing in which you desperately need His guidance?

DAY 3: How attuned are you to the Shepherd's voice? What keeps you from hearing Him clearly?
When have you found yourself on the right path but with the wrong attitude?
How does staying in the Word help you stay in His will? Share some specific examples.

DAY 4: How has God led you for His name's sake? What has brought Him glory along your path?

DAY 5: Share some of the highlights from your Green Pasture Day.
What is one significant truth you take away from this week of study?

If my written summary of this video teaching would be helpful to you, just go to *jenniferrothschild.com/psalm23* to get it.

WEEK 4

YOUR SHEPHERD IS BY YOUR SIDE

Yea, though I walk through the valley of the shadow of death, I will fear no evil; for You are with me; Your rod and Your staff, they comfort me.

PSALM 23:4

#PSALM23STUDY

DAY 1

Hey there! We're in Psalm 23:4 this week. So far, Psalm 23 has felt like a spiritual lullaby—soothing us, settling us, and helping us rest and be reassured.

But now, the lullaby slips into a minor key for a few bars. It's as if David slows down and lets us linger in the valley. Oh, how I wish there weren't a valley of the shadow of death in this psalm—in this life! But girl, valleys, shadows, and death are all realities we face, feel, and fear. Gratefully, we are promised our Shepherd's presence and comfort through all of it. So let's open His Word and learn how to live those truths.

I've got some hot tea, and I've lit my coffee candle—that's like being unequally yoked. (*Wink.*) I'm ready to study this with you. So settle in, sister, and let's linger with our Shepherd.

This week let's start by getting some dictionary definitions of the words to help us get a thorough look at the first part of this verse. Write the definitions below.

Walk:

Valley:

Shadow:

Death:

Fear:

Evil:

Review the definitions you wrote down. Consider how they deepen the meaning of verse 4. Then, write one big, long, amplified version of the first part of this verse using the definitions of the words, rather than the words themselves. (By the time you are done, you will have written one of those huge, paragraph long, apostle Paul kind of sentences!)

Here's an example: Yea though I (walk) advance, go one step at a time, travel by foot, navigate a certain path, move thoughtfully forward through the (valley) long depression in the surface of ...

OK, sister, that's all the help I'm going to give you. Hopefully you get the idea. Try it. And remember, there's not one right way to do this.

Linger over the amplified verse you wrote. Use it to praise and thank your Shepherd for His presence when life is dark. Worshiping and thanking God is a great way to open your heart and your study time in His Word. Quite honestly, this verse is so tender and stirring that you may discover it calls you to study your heart and your relationship with your Shepherd— even more than studying the verse itself.

Now, to the valley. All aboard!

THE VALLEY

When David wrote about the dark valleys or the valley of the shadow of death, he did so from two unique perspectives—two sources of experience. What do you think they were?

First, David knew the shepherd's perspective. He had led sheep through valleys in order to get them to greener pastures. He knew how timid the sheep could be when the valley was dark. He was familiar with the role of protector (1 Sam. 17:34-35).

Secondly, he also knew what it felt like to be a sheep, walking through the dark valleys of his own life. He knew how much he needed his Shepherd to lead him, comfort him, and help him get through. David understood both perspectives. That's one reason we need to pay attention to what he says in this verse. His words can help us be encouraged and assured as we face our own valleys. And we've all got dark valleys to go through, don't we?

"SHADOW OF DEATH"

Bible translators agree that the most accurate translation of the Hebrew for the phrase "shadow of death" is "darkest valleys."[1] The Hebrew word for this phrase is *sal-ma-wet* which means *dark shadows* or *darkness.*[2] But it shares the same Hebrew root for death (*ma-wet*), so it makes total sense why it was translated as "the shadow of death."[3]

There is the valley of depression and the valley of grief. There's the valley of rejection, the valley of divorce, and the valley of illness. There's the valley of stress, the valley of infertility, and the valley of longing, just to name a few. The point is that valleys foster fear and uncertainty. They are usually not places we want to tread alone. And when they get long, we need comfort.

So consider a valley you've already walked through or the one you're presently treading. Keep it in mind because we'll be referring back to it this week. Answer the questions below. (And if you are a multi-valley girl, that's OK. Write down all your valleys!)

If you're currently walking through a valley, what kind is it?

What is the most memorable valley you've walked through in the past?

What emotions rise in you as you walk through your valley?

What is your strongest memory from a past valley?

Valleys. You've got valleys; I've got valleys; all God's girls got valleys! And valleys aren't fun places to be, are they? But look at verse 4 again. How do we approach our valleys? (Hint: What is the verb before *through*?)

What does it mean to walk through something?

David is specific in using the words "walk through" because that phrase denotes movement and progress. We don't stop in the valley, buy a house, and live there forever. Valleys are conduits. They have an entrance and an exit. Valleys have a beginning. Valleys have an end. They are passages that take you from where you are to where you are going. With that thought in mind, journal your responses to the following.

What does it mean to walk through your valley rather than live in it?

What are the attitudes and actions of a woman who lives in rather than walks through her valley?

Do your attitudes and actions reflect that you are walking through or living in your valley? Explain.

What kinds of choices does a woman make when she understands her valley is a passage, not a permanent residence?

Do your choices reflect that you are using your valley as a passage or a permanent residence? Explain.

LIFE VERSE

Do you have a life verse? I'd love to hear it! If you're on Twitter, share your life verse and tag me (@JennRothschild). Be sure to share how the verse shapes your life perspective.

Sister, valleys are part of life's journey. And even when they last a long time, they are still temporary. Let me share with you my favorite verses, my life verses. They give me such hope and perspective when it comes to my own valleys. Read 2 Corinthians 4:16-18.

How does verse 17 describe our afflictions or troubles, our valleys?

Momentary. Temporary. It's kind of like our valleys are sticky notes on the refrigerator. They seem permanent. They may stick and stay for a long, long time. But after a while, they fall off. Our valleys may seem like they go on forever, but eventually, they will end.

That's how I feel about my blindness. Girl, it is a long dark valley, and some days it's all good—I'm walking by faith, smile on my face, leaning on my Shepherd. But then there are the deep dips, the potholes in my valley. Sometimes they last a day, sometimes months. When those low places come, they bring with them an emotional claustrophobia—blindness pushes in on me. The isolation feels so confining, heavy, and dark. But even though my blindness is terminal (unless God chooses to heal me on earth)—meaning it stays until the end—it is still temporary. Keeping the perspective that these troubles are momentary helps me continue to lean hard on my Shepherd and trust Him. But honestly, I still stumble a lot.

So if your valley is hard, ask God to give you grace to see your valleys through the lens of 2 Corinthians 4:17—temporary. Momentary. A blip on the radar. It will help you know that even what is most painful is not permanent in light of eternity.

My friend, we can't always change the valley we're in, but we can always change our attitudes, actions, and choices in that valley. When we walk through our valleys with our Shepherd, He uses the valleys to change us, to grow us, and to take us to a new and better place.

God can use our temporary valleys to create everlasting good for and in us.

Ask yourself the following questions and journal your responses.
Do I need to change my attitude about my valley? If so, how?

What different actions or choices could I make to change my experience in the valley?

What do I want my life on the other side of this valley to look like?

Now put down your pen and just be with your Shepherd. Review your responses. Ask His Spirit to lead you into truth, to help you understand and adjust your behavior if you need to.

David knew the sheep would fight fear every step of the way as the shepherd led them through the dark valley. But he led them anyway. Often the only way the shepherd could get sheep to new and better pastures was to take them through this dark valley. The shepherd led the sheep through what they feared in order to give them what they longed for and what they needed—a nourishing green pasture.

Sister, no matter your valley, it is not permanent. Your valley has purpose, and your valley is filled with God's presence. That's why we don't fear. In fact, we will talk about fear tomorrow. See you then!

DAY 2

I WILL FEAR NO EVIL

Easy to say, easy to type, easy to read, and easy to wear on your T-shirt. But when your valley lasts long and the darkness closes in—*bam!* Your fear gets real. At least this girl over here can get fearful in the valley. Sometimes I can feel fear just anticipating and dreading the valley that may or may not be in my future. It's taken me a while to admit and understand that about myself.

My dad's illness helped me face my fear about the valley of his death. I'm one of those blessed women who has a dad worthy of being called my hero. He is a rock, my rock. But when he almost died last year, I felt fear as I never had before. My dad made planet Earth safe and right. My dad made my world safe and right. And to think of him not being here made the whole world feel scary and wrong. I'm so grateful he made it through. But it awakened a fear in me—the fear that there will be a time when he doesn't make it through. And even though I know heaven is real and God's grace is sufficient, I still fight fear when the what-if starts to whisper. In fact, that is what I'm doing right now, even as I write this because he literally was just hospitalized again. I fear the loss. I fear the grief. I fear the what-if.

You've got your stuff too. You have a valley, or several, that whisper *what-if* to you. Fear is a natural reaction to our valleys. But, sister, faith is a supernatural response. We'll get to that response by the time we're done today, but first we've got to get honest about fear.

Some of us think we aren't fearful. However, fear shows up in ways we don't realize. Being overly controlling is fear in disguise. Anger is often fear in disguise. Isolating yourself is fear in disguise. Anxiety and worry are fear in disguise. (Well, those things aren't really good disguises!)

Think about your valley behavior. Does it reflect fear? If so, how is fear revealing itself? How is it affecting your trust in the Shepherd? Ask the Holy Spirit to guide you into truth and help you pinpoint the source of your fear. Give Him freedom to help you walk in faith, not fear. Stand on God's Word when it comes to fear.

Search your favorite Bible resource for Scriptures about not being afraid. Use words and phrases such as *fear*, *afraid*, *fear not*, and *don't be afraid* in your search. Add your references to the Scripture starters I've given below. Beside each reference, record what it says about not being afraid.

REFERENCE	WHAT THIS TELLS ME ABOUT FEAR
Joshua 1:9	
Psalm 56:3-4	
Isaiah 43:1	
2 Timothy 1:7	

Now use the encouragement and promises you found in the previous verses to create your personal declaration against fear. I've left you a spot on the next page. Or you can use the one I created for me—we can share! After you spend some time with your Shepherd reflecting on your statement, discuss it with one of your Bible study buddies. Chances are you are not the only sheep who deals with fear.

MY *FEAR NOT* PROCLAMATION

My Shepherd didn't give me
the spirit of fear (2 Tim. 1:7).
My heart does not have to be
troubled or fearful because my
Good Shepherd gives me peace
(John 14:27). His love chases fear
away (1 John 4:18). When my
anxious thoughts grow within me,
my Shepherd's comfort
gives me joy instead (Ps. 94:19).
I don't need to be afraid because
I belong to my Shepherd
(Isa. 43:1). I can leave my worries
with Him because He cares for me
(1 Pet. 5:7). I don't have to fear.
I can have faith (Mark 5:36).

YOUR *FEAR NOT* PROCLAMATION

Now, let's get one thing straight right here, right now. Just because you feel fear doesn't mean you can't have faith at the same time. Fear and faith can share the same heartbeat. Find Mark 9:21-24. As you read about a Dad whose son needed healing, meditate on his response to Jesus in verse 24. If you are in a valley and you're fighting fear, write down Mark 9:24 as your prayer for the valley.

Lord, I believe. Help my unbelief.

Sister, I get it. I know that even when we have faith, it's so easy to feel fear when the shadows of uncertainty get thick.

But even though fear and faith can share the same heartbeat, they don't share the same perspective. That's why we need the faith perspective when it comes to our valleys.

Fear focuses on the shadows. Faith focuses on the Shepherd.

Fear sees only the dark of the valley. Faith sees the light of the Shepherd. So how do we get the faith perspective? How do we see our valleys, our very lives, through the eyes of faith?

When I went to Scripture with this question, I found these two ways to get the faith perspective. Let's look at them together.

    1. How does Romans 10:17 say we get the faith perspective?

We hear His Word. We read His Word. God's Word produces faith. Our opinions and speculations will not produce faith. Instead they can easily produce fear. So girl, if we want to have the faith perspective, we've got to stay in His Word. Does it seem that no matter what we study, it leads back to this truth? There is just no substitute for God's Word!

    2. How does Luke 17:5 suggest we get the faith perspective?

The apostles asked Jesus to increase their faith and so can we. Want more faith? Ask Him for it. Faith is a gift that God gives us. When we ask Him for more, He gives us what we need.

Sister, even the darkest valleys aren't so dark when God is with us. He is light (1 John 1:5), and His Word is a light to our paths (Ps. 119:105). So ask Him for faith, and stay in His Word. Your faith will grow, and you will see light even when your valley is dark.

As we finish up, spend some quiet moments with your Shepherd.

Pour some coffee or tea, and linger with Him. If your walk through the valley feels a little wobbly, ask Him for faith. Tell Him you believe, and ask Him to help your unbelief. Ask Him to help you recognize your fear and increase your faith. He loves you, my sister. You are His precious lamb, and He wants you to feel His comfort and presence in your valley.

Here's the last thing I want to remind you of today: valley times don't last but valiant women do!

Yep. Take that, fear! We may feel fear from time to time, but we are the women of God who are strong and courageous in our Lord!

Fear not! See you tomorrow.

DAY 3

YOU ARE WITH ME

OK, at this point, we get it. We don't need to fear the dark or the shadow of death.

But why not? What does the verse say?

Was David unafraid because the valley was shallow? Did his calmness come because he had great valley walking insurance or exceptional valley management skills? Was his fear abated because his faith was huge? No.

The reason David did not fear is the same reason you and I don't have to be afraid—our Shepherd is with us. It's not that danger is absent but that God is present.

You listed several Scripture passages yesterday that talked about fear and why we don't have to be afraid. Review those verses and look up all of the following that are not on yesterday's list.

Psalm 27:1 • Psalm 46:1-2 • Proverbs 3:25-26 • Isaiah 35:4
Isaiah 41:10-14 • Matthew 28:20 • 1 John 4:18

I love all these verses, don't you? So comforting. Such confidence builders.

Based on these verses, I made a list of all the reasons I don't need to be fearful. When my feelings tell me to be afraid, I review my list. It helps me keep a faith perspective.

Since we all fight and face fears from time to time, create your own list. But, instead of just making a list, write the reasons all over the walls of the valley image below. Girl, this is like grace graffiti!

REASONS I DON'T NEED TO FEAR

You know why we wrote on the walls of the valley? Because it represents something significant. When someone uses the phrase, "the writing is on the wall," it's like hearing that ominous "da, da, da, da, dom" music right before the main bad guy gets clobbered in a video game. It means something is about to fail or no longer exist. So when you put the reasons not to be afraid on the wall, you are reminding yourself that fear will fail because faith and truth are more powerful. Yes!

All the reasons you wrote on the wall are true for you today, and they will be true for you tomorrow also. They will be true for you for a thousand tomorrows. Why? Because they're based on God's Word, and His Word stands forever. Oh, thank You, Lord!

My friend, nothing you fear is more powerful than your God. Struggling with fear is universal, but what makes us afraid can be unique and personal. God's presence is also unique and personal. David wrote, "You are with me" (Ps. 23:4). You. Me. That means your Shepherd is with you in this moment. His presence is personal. He's able to meet you right where you are. Notice how many verses connect not being afraid with God being present. His light dispels the darkness.

Go back and read Psalm 23:1-3, and notice the pronouns you find in each.

Verse 1 pronouns:

Verse 2 pronouns:

Verse 3 pronouns:

Now how do the pronouns change in verse 4?

Verse 4 pronouns:

You may want to circle the pronouns in verse 4 because they are absolutely beautiful. *You. Your.* David shifts from talking *about* His Shepherd to talking *to* His Shepherd. Why do you think the shift occurs in this verse?

God gets personal when the valley gets dark.

Now we know that God is always a personal God, in all ways and all occasions. However, sometimes it's those valley experiences that move us from knowing about our Shepherd to really knowing our Shepherd.

With your valley (or valleys) in mind, answer the following questions.

What have you learned (or what are you learning) about your Shepherd when life was (or is) the darkest?

How did you (or do you) experience your Shepherd in a personal way while in the valley?

God's presence is a fact, but let's be real—it isn't always a feeling. At least not for me.

We need to remember that faith isn't based on feeling. Faith is grounded in the truth of God's Word and the integrity of His character. He has promised to be with us through all things, and God never breaks a promise. So although you may not feel God's presence, you can absolutely know and trust that He is there.

However, when you are in that valley and you feel alone, here are some ways to help you recognize His presence. These will help you focus on the fact of His presence rather than your feeling of fear.

1. BE STILL

Read Psalm 46:10. Stillness increases our awareness of His presence. Often our response to valleys is to run frantically, worry incessantly, and look for the nearest off-ramp. When this happens, stop. Pray. Ask the Lord to help you be still, to listen, and to quiet your heart. I suggest you don't wait for valley moments for this practice. Take five minutes every day, and just be still with Him. Read Scripture out loud. Why out loud? Because speaking His Word and hearing His Word require stillness and focus.

I've been quoting Psalm 23 over and over to help me be still and focus on my Shepherd. In fact, I did it just now. I was interrupted with a phone call about my dad, and immediately, my fear factor started to rise! Girl, speaking and meditating on this psalm helped me be still. And the more I quoted it, I began to pray it and use it to praise my Shepherd. Six times— that's how many times I quoted it in five minutes. Try it. And let me know how God's living and active Word made you aware of His presence with you. Your focus on the valley diminishes when you're focusing on quoting Scripture. Sister, you are not alone. Get still so you can know He is with you.

2. SING PRAISE

Yep, sing. Find Psalm 22:3 to see why. God really is present in and situated within your praise. He inhabits and resides in. You don't have to be a good singer or a loud singer (especially if you aren't a good singer). But when you sing, every note builds a throne and God rushes in to sit on it. Worship is the way you draw near to God.

According to James 4:8, what happens when you draw near?

You will sense His nearness in your valley when you call on His Name, praise Him, and are still before Him.

God is with you in your valley.

My friend, sometimes it is very difficult to clearly see the lessons we need to learn and how deeply we are loved and cared for while we are navigating the valley. Sometimes we have to get through it to understand what we got from it. So if you are in the dark middle of your valley, don't press to find the grand lesson or insight if one is not clear. Just rest in your Shepherd. Let Him carry you through. Receive His comfort and care.

Eventually, you will get to verse 5 where there will be a lovely table waiting for you. At that point, you can look back with clarity while you enjoy the banquet of blessing that God is preparing for you even now.

Sheep didn't like walking through what they couldn't see. The shepherd had to be mindful that bandits and bad guys could be waiting in those shadows to pounce on him and steal the sheep. But the sheep needed not fear because the shepherd was with them. The shepherd needed not fear because he had his rod and staff. And that, my friend, is my not so subtle segue into what we will talk about tomorrow! So until then, may you feel the presence of your Shepherd every remaining moment of this day.

DAY 4

YOUR ROD AND YOUR STAFF, THEY COMFORT ME

Comfort. Ah, one of my favorite words. What comes to mind when you think of comfort?

I think of food! I try not to, but pizza, vegetable soup, or my mom's pound cake fill my thoughts. I also think of a warm blanket by the fire and the fragrance of vanilla. So before I continue typing, I'm going to move over by my fireplace and light a vanilla candle. (I wish I had some comfort food to go along with it!)

How about you do the same? Go to that place in your home or in your heart where you enjoy the most comfort. Once we're all settled here, let's think about how we feel when we are comforted or comfortable. What words come to mind?

Safe. Secure. Relaxed. Peaceful. Those are some words that come to my mind when I think of comfort. But girl, you want to know what two words that would never come to my mind? Rod and staff. Those things don't sound nearly as comforting as pound cake or a warm blanket! But David, the shepherd, told the Lord, His Shepherd, that it was the rod and staff that brought him comfort.

Why?

Let's check out other places rods and staffs show up in Scripture and what they represent.

First, do a word search on *rod*, and try to determine, within the context, what rods may represent. Depending on the version you use the words *rods* and *staffs* may appear to be interchangeable. See if you can determine the reason.

REFERENCE	WHAT THIS VERSE TELLS ME ABOUT A *ROD* AND *STAFF*
Numbers 17	
Job 21:9	
Proverbs 29:15	

When a man held a rod, it represented authority. It was a tool of discipline and showed that he had the ability and readiness to defend. Also a rod represented honor and fruitfulness.

Based on the Scriptures you found or the Scripture starters, how does God's rod (His authority, His discipline, His protection) bring you comfort when you are in a dark valley?

God's authority brings me comfort because:

God's discipline brings me comfort because:

God's protection brings me comfort because:

God's gentle guidance and discipline make us feel safe in our valleys. God's willingness and ability to defend and protect us give us confidence to keep walking.

We feel comforted in our valleys because God has authority over them. The darkness won't last one minute longer than He decides.

We need to remember that David was a rod- and staff-toting shepherd who wrote this verse to the Lord who was his Shepherd. Let's take a look at a passage of Scripture that will give us context for David penning these words in Psalm 23.

> Read 1 Samuel 17:34-35. How did David, the shepherd, react when one of his sheep was in danger? Did he mildly observe? Did he panic and run? Did he drop and pray?

No, sister! David turned into a one-man, rod-swinging wrecking crew! He went after the beast, fought ferociously, and rescued his lamb. And if the unfortunate beast was dumb enough to fight back during this rescue, David would grab it by the throat and then *wham*. Call the taxidermist. That's all she wrote.

If I have that guy looking out for me, I am feeling quite safe. How about you? There is no greater comfort than to know that someone will protect you, fight for you, and rescue you—risk his very life for you. That is the description of your Good Shepherd.

Girl, I need to pause and just receive this truth. You do too. Put down your pen and any other burden you're carrying right now and just receive His authority, His discipline, and His protection.

> Look up the verses listed next to each prayer to help you truly receive the comfort God wants to give you. Make these passages a part of your prayers.
>
> **LORD, I RECEIVE YOUR AUTHORITY.** Psalm 115:3; Matthew 28:18; John 3:35; Colossians 2:10

Use this space to journal your thoughts and prayers concerning God's authority, discipline, and protection over your life.

LORD, I RECEIVE YOUR DISCIPLINE. Job 5:17; Psalm 94:12; Proverbs 3:12

LORD, I RECEIVE YOUR PROTECTION. Exodus 14:14; Deuteronomy 3:22; Deuteronomy 20:4; Nahum 1:7; Romans 8:31

The Lord is your shepherd. His rod comforts you.

Now, find *staff* in a Bible dictionary or Bible encyclopedia. Remember, BibleStudyTools.com is a great resource.

Based on what you found, how do the rod and staff differ?

Do you think the rod and staff serve different purposes? If so, how?

OK sister, this part may have gotten a little fuzzy for you; it did for me. Let me give you the Hebrew words for *rod* and *staff*, in case you didn't find them. It should help clarify the meaning of these words. The Hebrew word for *rod* is *shebet,* and it has the idea of a stick. It originally referred to a part of a tree. And we already discovered its uses.[4] On the other hand—literally, in the shepherd's other hand—was the staff. The Hebrew word for *staff* is *mishenah,* and it carries the thought of something to lean on, trust, support.[5]

When it came to sheep, the shepherd used the rod to firmly guide and protect the flock, and he used the staff to draw the sheep to himself and keep them close. Both actions of the shepherd brought the sheep comfort because they felt secure, safe, and seen by their shepherd.

That is why we can feel safe with our Shepherd too. We are secure in Him, safe with Him, and seen by Him every single day of our lives. What comfort that is!

Let's finish up today with the word *comfort*.

Find the definition for *comfort* in the dictionary, and write it here.

The verb form of *comfort* means to give emotional strength to someone.[7]

If you're super ambitious, find the etymology (history of the word), and note how it deepens your understanding of the way God gives us emotional strength in our valleys.

ETYMOLOGY HOW-TO

Etymology is defined by *Merriam-Webster's Dictionary* as "the history of a linguistic form (such as a word) shown by tracing its development since its earliest recorded occurrence in the language where it is found, by tracing its transmission from one language to another, by analyzing it into its component parts, by identifying its cognates in other languages, or by tracing it and its cognates to a common ancestral form in an ancestral language."[6] In short, it's the history of a word. Discovering the history of the word can provide important insight into its meaning. This is especially helpful when exploring the meaning of biblical words. To find the history and meaning of biblical words, use reference books such as *Strong's Exhaustive Concordance* or *Vine's Expository Dictionary*. Bible apps such as WordSearch and Logos can also be good sources.

We receive ultimate comfort through God's presence.

Do you need comfort? To be with God and made strong by Him?

Sometimes we seek comfort in all the wrong places. Food, drink, activity, status, escape from the valley—none of those things give us ultimate comfort or strength. They don't provide the companionship our souls crave.

Take a moment to evaluate if God is the true source of comfort for you. Ask Him to show you. Look back at the beginning of this day's study when I asked you what words come to mind when you feel comforted or comfortable. Jot them here again.

Are those the feelings you have in your valley, walking with your Shepherd? Those emotions will help you evaluate whether or not you're receiving God's comfort. If not, turn your heart back to the Lord, and seek His true comfort and peace. Don't settle for temporary solutions when the comforting Shepherd is by your side.

Last thought for today—for this week: When we are comforted sheep, we can comfort other sheep. We can be the ones God uses to strengthen other valley-walking women.

The Latin root of the word *fort* in comfort means *strong*.[8] When we comfort others, it is as if God uses us to help turn the weak and broken pieces of someone's life into a fortress of God's strength once again.

Girl, you can be that woman. However, if you're the one in need of comfort, to be put back together and made strong, stay in the flock. Be honest. Tell a Bible study buddy. Sister, when we get real, we get well!

Why settle for less? In our Shepherd, we lack nothing. So let's receive everything our Shepherd gives us.

Thank You, Lord, for Your comfort. Thank You for Your presence. Thank You for light in our valleys and peace in our chaos. Thank You that You have authority over our valleys and You will use them to bring us to better places with You. Amen.

This little verse is so big with truth—I feel like we barely put a dent in it. But sometimes we have to quit before we're done, and this is one of those times.

I'm loving studying this psalm with you, my friend. I pray God pulls all the pieces of this verse together for you in a very unique and personal way as you spend a Green Pasture Day with Him tomorrow.

See you on video!

DAY 5

GREEN PASTURE DAY: A DAY TO REST AND DIGEST

Yea, though I walk through the valley of the shadow

of death, I will fear no evil; for You are with me;

Your rod and Your staff, they comfort me.

PSALM 23:4

As you use this day to do whatever helps you digest what you've learned this week, consider that Psalm 23:4 helps us understand the Presence Principle: You are never alone because your Shepherd never leaves you.

On your Green Pasture Day, as you rest, pray, journal, draw, worship, or ponder, here are some things to consider:

Scriptures I want to remember from this week:

Quotes I liked from this week:

Someone I need to comfort, to be with, to help make strong:

Verses about fear I want to remember:

To help you walk through your valley with joy, listen to the songs I included in my *Psalm 23* playlist at JenniferRothschild.com/Psalm23.

Thank You, Lord, for walking with me and comforting me in my valleys.

GROUP SESSION 5

BEFORE THE VIDEO

Welcome and Prayer

VIDEO NOTES

Three Valleys We Go Through

1. The Valley of Baca represents weeping, _____, and sadness.

TWO THINGS YOU CAN DO WHEN YOU ARE IN THE VALLEY OF BACA

    1. Make the Lord your _____.

        When we are not honest, our Valley of Baca will be a lot _____ and last a lot _____.

    2. Set your heart on _____.

        When you are passing through the Valley of Baca, hold onto your _____, take one step at a _____, and _____.

2. The Valley of Elah is the valley of _____.
   - Battles rarely _____. Most often they _____ up.

   - When we are in the valley of battle, we can forget who the real _____ is.

   - Every battle we _____ belongs to the Lord.

   - When you are in the valley, you need to _____ _____.

3. The Valley of Achor
   - The Valley of Achor is a place of deep _____ and often a place of _____.

   - If you are in the Valley of Achor, when you look for the _____ of _____, everything will change.

#PSALM23STUDY

- When you are in the Valley of Achor, you can become a door of hope for _____ _____.

CONVERSATION GUIDE
Video 5

DAY 1: What are some valleys that you have personally faced over the last few years? What was your experience of walking through these valleys? Was it just a passage or did you camp out in the valley?

DAY 2: How did you deal with fear during your time in the valley? On a scale of 1-10, with 1 being *Consumed by Fear* and 10 being *Walked by Faith*, how would you rank yourself? Explain your ranking.
Share with the group your "Fear Not" proclamation.

DAY 3: What are some of the reasons not to be afraid that you wrote on your valley wall? How did you experience the Lord's presence in your valley season? How did His presence become more personal during that time?

DAY 4: How did God comfort you during your valley experience? How are you doing at comforting those sisters around you who are walking through the valley? Who do you know that needs to be comforted and encouraged? What will you do to minister to them?

DAY 5: Share some of the highlights from your Green Pasture Day. What is one significant truth you take away from this week of study?

I bet you know someone who would be encouraged by this video teaching. Get my written summary of this message at jenniferrothschild.com/Psalm23.

YOUR SHEPHERD CALLS YOU HIS

You prepare a table before me in
the presence of my enemies;
You anoint my head with
oil; my cup runs over.

PSALM 23:5

#PSALM23STUDY

DAY 1

This week, the table is set and the celebration begins! So get out your favorite cup and saucer because Word has it your cup is about to overflow. And you, sister, will be sipping from the saucer!

So far in Psalm 23, we've rested in green pastures and sat beside still waters. We've walked down right paths and tiptoed (or been dragged, kicking and screaming) through dark valleys. Just like it is in our lives, these verses have taken us through situations and seasons. But we haven't had a season of celebration—until now.

This verse (Ps. 23:5) doesn't suggest that life will feel like one big happy dance every single day, but it does point out that there will always be table times of blessing and joy. They happen more than we may think—even in the valleys! We need to recognize and receive them as gifts and signs of our Shepherd's ultimate plan for us.

So wash your hands; it's time for dinner—and you don't even have to set the table.

YOU PREPARE A TABLE BEFORE ME

Are you sitting at your table right now? We all have our favorite places to study, read, think, and pray. For you it may be a rocker on your deck or a recliner near the fireplace. It may be at your desk or in a coffee shop. Or you may feel coziest at your kitchen table. That's where I'm sitting, right here with my laptop and a cup of coffee.

But even if you're not reading this at your table, you've got one, right? Most of us have a table, and it's the place we eat.

> Take a good look at your table. How many seats are there? Usually more than one, right? Why is that? What is the purpose of a dining table with many chairs?

Tables are places we gather—a place we spend time together. Think about occasions you've spent at your table or other special tables, eating with people you love.

When I look back at table times in my life, I think of summer dinners at my Southern auntie's home with her beautiful blue-rimmed china and fresh tomatoes from her garden. I think of Christmas dinner on Mama's and Papa's antique table with squeaky chairs and summer fish frys at Granddaddy's picnic table overlooking the Apalachicola River.

I remember how my mom always set the most beautiful holiday table with lace, fresh flowers, and all the family heirloom silver. (Her pound cake is unmatched to this very day!) I also cherish those pizza-on-paper-plate times on my smudged glass table with my boys while VeggieTales® played in the background. Table times for me are happy, meaningful, special, deep, tender, precious, connected, fun, safe, honest, and life-giving.

What are some words and feelings that come to your mind when you remember your own times at the table? Make a list here.

TABLE TIMES EXPERIENCES	TABLE TIMES EMOTIONS

Table time experiences are usually flush with emotions. Is that what your lists indicate? The Scripture also contains several mentions about times around the table. Use your favorite online resource or the concordance in the back of your Bible to find verses with the word *table* in Scripture. Look for other words associated with tables such as *feast, banquet,* and *eat* to broaden your search.

List the references below, including the kind of table it is, the purpose of the gathering, and which of your Table Times emotions from the previous list fits that particular table.

TABLE REFERENCE	TABLE TYPE	TABLE EMOTION
2 Samuel 9:1-7		
1 Kings 2:7		
Isaiah 25:6-9		
Matthew 22:1-4		
Luke 14:15		

It's not just us! For thousands of years, tables have been the gathering places, the depositories, the launching pads for so many of life's most precious times. Joy, pondering, celebration, hospitality, honor, and blessing are just a few of the experiences at the table we see in Scripture.

So think of this eating at the table concept in the context of Psalm 23. Have you ever seen a sheep eating from a table? I doubt it! So why does David describe the Lord, our Shepherd, preparing a table before us—for us, His sheep? This would be a good question to Google or research in a commentary. But if you want me to just tell you, I will. *Spoiler alert! Spoiler alert!* Don't read the next paragraph until you find the answer yourself, if you want to.

David wrote this psalm about his Shepherd as if he, David, was a sheep. But, surprise! In verse 5, he shifts the image from God as a shepherd to God as a generous host or God as a king throwing a banquet celebration.

> Why does David describe the Lord, our Shepherd, preparing a table before us—for us, His sheep?

What is this table like? In ancient Hebrew banquet tradition, a king or wealthy, benevolent host would invite the important and favored people to his table. Often the grand feast would be held outside so all the people could see who was at the party—and who was not. The king's favor was obvious to everyone who looked on—including any defeated enemies, grumpy neighbors, or jealous mean girls. (Those last two are just what I imagine.) So the table was a place of blessing, favor, and communion.

In a figurative sense, God's table is His favor, blessing, and communion extended to us. It's an invitation to partake of the good things of God. It's an opportunity to accept God's provision, experience His protection, and enjoy His pleasure.

How do you see God's "table" evident in your life?

In verse 5, who prepares this table?

In David's context, who do you think normally prepared the table?

Who prepares the table for guests in your context?

Unless you're married to a professional chef or a guy who just loves to cook and throw dinner parties, you are probably the one who prepares the meal and the table. And you are the one who likely serves the guests. (If it's me we're talking about, though, it would be me and Papa John—he's my caterer!)

In ancient Hebrew culture, a servant would have prepared the meal and the table, not the host. What does that fact say about the character of your Shepherd King and your value as a sheep?

Girl, it is just flat-out radical that God prepares the table for us. God the Host serves the guests. God the Shepherd serves the sheep. God the Father serves the children. God the King serves His subjects. It should be exactly the opposite, right? We should be preparing a table for Him, not the other way around. **We love and are loved by such a humble God.**

Keeping this picture in mind, read Philippians 2:6-8 and identify four examples that affirm Jesus as the One who serves us at the table. List them below with the reference.

Servant examples of Jesus in Philippians 2:

1.

2.

3.

4.

Or you can write out Philippians 2:6-8 in the space provided and circle the qualities in the verses themselves. Writing Scripture helps reinforce it in our minds and hearts.

Think about it. If you chose to risk your reputation for someone, if you gave up your right to be served and chose to serve instead, if you identified with the lowest of the low, if you humbled yourself on behalf of someone else and that humility meant ultimate sacrifice, what would your behavior and choices be communicating?

Evidently the object of your actions must be incredibly valuable to you. Just think, Jesus did that—does that—for you and me! What emotions well up in you when you consider what Jesus has done for you? Pause and tell Him. Express your wonder and gratefulness and praise to Him for valuing you in such a way. Write out a prayer to your Shepherd thanking Him for His loving desire to treat you with such honor.

Dear Lord,

Amen.

Oh girl, this truth is so rich and so humbling. I've got to refill my coffee and just pause here to let this sink in.

YOUR RESPONSE TO THE TABLE

Let's shift gears. Imagine you actually received an invitation to the Psalm 23:5 table, and you need to RSVP to let your Host know you will be there. Write a note to your Shepherd Host thanking Him for the invitation. In your note, tell Him how you feel about being invited and what you look forward to experiencing when you sit at His table. Use the words you listed under Table Times Emotions earlier to influence and inform the content of your RSVP.

    MY RSVP:

The RSVP indicates your desire to receive your Shepherd King's blessing, favor, and communion. You are saying to the Lord, "I accept what You provide for me. I am already experiencing and will continue to experience Your presence and protection. I am excited and ready to enjoy Your pleasure."

This week, practice starting each day with an RSVP. Thank your Shepherd for saving you a seat at His table, and tell Him you are ready to receive what He has prepared for you. Be aware of His provision, presence, protection, and pleasure all day long.

Here's a good way to help you live out your RSVP and intentionally experience table times this week. Take four index cards or sticky notes and title them:

☐ Provision Sightings
☐ Protection Sightings
☐ Presence Sightings
☐ Pleasure Sightings

Carry them with you throughout each day, and ask your Shepherd to make you aware of how He is providing, protecting, and honoring you with His presence and pleasure. When you notice God's blessing, record it on the correct card or note. Just use a few words, ones that will jog your memory. At the end of the week, attach your notes or cards on your Green Pasture Day so you can review.

Let me give you some personal examples.

PROVISION SIGHTING—LIGHT THERAPY BOX

I saw my Shepherd's provision in this handy gadget that was shipped to my home this week. I learned about how its bright light mimics natural outdoor sunshine. Evidently light therapy can affect brain chemicals associated with sleep and mood.

I've been struggling with insomnia and depression, and I learned it could be from my eyes not processing light very well—kind of like Seasonal Affective Disorder every day of the year. So I've put it on my desk to shine a light of hope! The light therapy box is just another way God is caring for me—it's His provision.

PRESENCE SIGHTING—JOHN 16:33

This morning while listening to John 16, I felt my Shepherd's nearness and heard His voice reassuring me that He was speaking to me, telling me He had overcome the world and I could have peace in Him.

PLEASURE SIGHTING—QUINOA & KALE BOWL

This food made for a delicious lunch! It made me think of how good God is to give such interesting and pleasurable foods, just for me to enjoy.

Get the idea? Oh sister, do it, really. It will help you expect and experience table times all day long and all week long.

You know what really blows my mind? Our invitation to the table has nothing to do with our merit. It has absolutely nothing to do with what we bring to the table. Our invitation is based on our Shepherd King's grace—His character and His choice.

God's character sets the table, and His grace saves you a seat.

So when you RSVP, just plan to show up. God has already provided what you need to wear. What does Isaiah 61:10 say about your wardrobe?

My sister, when you received Christ, the old was made new. The filthy rags you used to think were the latest fashion were replaced with brand new robes of righteousness! You woke up this morning fully dressed in the garment of salvation so you are ready to sit at His table—you fit right in! His blessing, favor, and presence are prepared for you. So pull up a chair.

And not only does He serve us at the table. He does it in the face of our enemies. By now, you know that was my way of saying "stay tuned"!

DAY 2

IN THE PRESENCE OF MY ENEMIES

Enemies. What a way to start a day.

> So who do you think the enemies are in this verse? Evidently, for David, there was more than one. If David has shifted the imagery from shepherd to king and host, what enemies could he have in mind?

David could have been holed up in a cave thinking of Ahithophel or Absalom when he pondered enemies. Thoughts of those men, one a friend and the other his son, could have been fresh and tender on his mind. Or he could have been thinking of armies like the Philistines or the

> For context, note that David likely wrote this psalm while in Mahanaim. Read 2 Samuel 17 and refer to your Week 2 video notes for additional insights.

Geshurites, Girzites, and the Amalekites. (Or any of the other dozen "ites" I can't pronounce!) He had plenty of enemies to choose from.

David faced quite a few enemies in his life—wild animals, a jealous king, a giant, a former friend, and more. He knew what it felt like to be threatened, hated, and treated with hostility.

Perhaps you also have enemies. Maybe specific people even came to mind. But we're not just talking about human enemies. Sure, people hurt us and oppose us. Sometimes we may even endure a long-lasting, hostile relationship. And sometimes there are people who are just plain ugly and mean. But let's find out a little more about this word *enemies* to fully understand what we're dealing with.

The Hebrew word for *enemies* in this verse suggests to vex or show *hostility*. Vex. Not a word I use a lot. Like never. So I looked it up. Why don't you do the same?

> Find it in a dictionary, and then jot down the definition here.

One definition I found for *vex* means "to disturb the peace of mind."[1]

How does an enemy seek to disturb an opponent's peace of mind?

What disturbs your peace of mind?

Conflict disturbs my peace of mind. Stress disturbs my peace of mind, big time. Did I say disturb? I meant destroys. When I think of what disturbs my peace of mind, sometimes it may be mean words spoken to me or about me, but mostly, it is my circumstances. Stressful ones. You know, when I think about it, stress or conflict can become enemies to my soul.

How about you? How do those things that disturb your peace of mind become enemies to your soul?

There are situations, circumstances, and even people that vex us. But read Ephesians 6:12. Who does Paul says the enemy is *not*?

How many people fit into this "flesh and blood" category? All of them. That means that the parade of disagreeables who disturb your peace of mind—who may behave as enemies—are not really enemies at all. Perhaps they are just weapons in the hand of the real enemy. Hmmm—even stress, conflict, or whatever else you wrote on your list can be tools in the hand of the real enemy too. So think about the real enemy.

Who is the real enemy of your soul and how does Scripture describe him and his ways? Find some verses that describe Satan, and list the references along with words that describe him. Write this list under the headline, *Enemy Slime*. (Yes, I wrote slime!) Once you finish your list, compare it to the list you made yesterday under Table Times Emotions. Do some of the same words appear on both lists? Are they different? How?

ENEMY SLIME

REFERENCES	ENEMY NAMES & DESCRIPTIONS
Genesis 3:1	
Zechariah 3:1	
Matthew 4:1	
Matthew 16:23	
John 8:44	
John 10:10	
Ephesians 6:11	
1 Peter 5:8	
Revelation 12:9	

Your enemy is a crafty accuser, a filthy liar. He's a scheming stumbling block who seeks to devour your joy, kill your confidence, steal your hope, and tempt you to believe that his way of living and thinking is better than your Shepherd's. Yuck. I think I need to wash my hands after typing all that slime.

When you compared Table Times Emotions with Enemy Slime, did you see how none of the slime describing your enemy is part of the table times you described yesterday? Girl, the point is there should be no enemy slime with your table time. God prepares a table before you, and it is in front of your enemy not *with* your enemy!

If you feel like you experience more enemy slime than spiritual blessings of table times, then maybe you have pulled up an extra chair and given your enemy a seat at the table. In other words, you're letting the enemy mess with the blessing, favor, and communion you have with and from your Shepherd.

Stop and evaluate. Have you given your enemy a seat at the table? Are you experiencing the favor, blessing, and companionship God has prepared just for you? Or is the enemy spoiling the banquet? Pause here and really think and pray about this—just you and your Shepherd.

Let's switch gears for a moment. We'll come back to the enemy's intrusion, but sometimes we need to realize our banquet with the Shepherd is interrupted because we wrongly assume there will just be days, times, and seasons when we won't experience the table. The enemy doesn't need a seat to disrupt our feasting because we've already given up our own seat. We don't RSVP to God's invitation. We've decided we're not even going to show up. Oh sister, I get it.

There are valley times when we truly grieve and life is hard. As I said yesterday, life isn't always just one big happy dance.

But even in the valley, even when life is hard, that doesn't mean God can't or won't prepare a table right there. In fact, I have a verse you will love.

Find Psalm 78:19. What were the wilderness-wandering Israelites questioning about God?

GO DEEPER

Read Psalm 78:20. There you'll find the Israelites answer their own doubts about God. He, in fact, can provide—even in the wilderness. How did He do it? Water came out of a rock! Can you imagine? So contrary to how the Israelites responded, trust Him. See how He's been faithful in the past, and trust Him to be faithful in the future. I'm so thankful that even when life is difficult God is right there with me, making Himself known and preparing a table.

"Can God prepare a table in the wilderness?" The Israelites had been wandering in the wilderness, and in their rebellious hearts, they just couldn't imagine or accept that God would provide for and protect them. They doubted His power, His goodness, and His character. They didn't expect to enjoy His pleasure. No way, not there.

But the Shepherd's power and goodness are not limited by difficult times. Even in the valley He can set us a table. Oh sister, I'm learning I can still come to the table every day and be happy in Jesus—even when life is hard. OK, back to the enemy.

THE ENEMY IS NOT INVITED

If you're not sure if you've given Satan a seat at your table, look again at the Enemy Slime— the Scripture-based list and description you wrote about Satan.

> How does his ugly activity show up in your life and disturb your peace of mind?

He steals my ...

He lies about ...

He kills my ...

He accuses me of ...

He deceives me into thinking ...

He tries to destroy ...

If you determine Satan is trying to sneak a seat at your table and steal all the blessings, uninvite him. Earlier you sent an RSVP to your Shepherd King concerning the invitation to His table. Now, write an "uninvitation" to your enemy. Tell him why he is not allowed at your table and include the Scriptures below to explain why he can't come.

Isaiah 54:17 • Romans 8:31 • 1 John 4:4 • Revelation 12:11

My "Uninvitation" to Satan:

Sometimes we don't even realize that Satan has pulled up a chair. So ask the Lord to make you aware of your real enemy. Ask Him to turn up the volume so you can hear what chatter you are listening to.

If your thoughts are condemning, accusatory, bitter, hopeless, dark, or ugly, girl, it's time to send an uninvite. If your mind and heart are filled with lies and accusations about the character of God and who you are in Him, that is the voice of your enemy. He is not allowed to sit at the table. If he stays, he will steal the blessing, delight, and joy your Shepherd is serving you.

God's words to you will line up with Galatians 5:22-23—words of love, joy, peace, patience, kindness, goodness, faithfulness, gentleness, and self-control (NASB). Anything that disagrees with that sweet Holy Spirit fruit doesn't come from your Shepherd. Think of it this way, the fruit of the Spirit is always on the menu.

God prepares a table for you because He loves you and wants to bless and celebrate you. Don't let the enemy steal the abundance. Listen for the voice of your Shepherd. His voice is truth.

Oh, thank You, Lord!

DAY 3

YOU ANOINT MY HEAD WITH OIL

I'm back at my table again today, sitting here waiting for you! It just seems right that we should hang out at the table this week while we're learning about the table God prepares for us.

At my table, there are always a few things guaranteed to happen. First, coffee. Most of my people love their coffee, so rarely is there a gathering at my table without coffee. Secondly, and this one is quirky, napkins. Yes! I am really into napkins. They don't have to be fancy or cloth, but there just needs to be a napkin at each place setting—especially at mine. I can't even take my first bite without a napkin in my lap or in my hand.

What about you? What is always a part of your table?

David says there are two things that happen at the table the Lord prepares. Read or quote the verse again to remind yourself of what they are. Write them here in first person.

What happens at the table the Lord prepares?

1.

2.

That's right! One: God anoints my head with oil. Two: my cup runs over.

I really do want to know what is always a part of your table! Tweet me at @JennRothschild, and let me know. Or take a pic and Instagram it with #Psalm23Study so we can all get to know each other. Besides, I want to know how quirky you are too!

Let's start with the anointing.

Lord, lead us into truth today. Help us understand who You are and Your kind intentions toward us. Protect Your Word and help us to understand what it really means to experience Your anointing. Amen.

OK, sister, let's start with a Scripture word search. Find verses that use the words *anoint*, *anoint with oil*, or any form of the words. Then based on those verses, describe what you think is the purpose and result of being anointed with oil. I've included some Scripture starters.

Leviticus 8:12 • 1 Samuel 16:13 • Isaiah 61:1 • Luke 7:46
Acts 10:38 • James 5:14 • 1 John 2:20,27 • _____
_____ • _____ • _____

Purposes of Anointing:

Results of Anointing:

Hopefully, you were able to sort through all the verses and narrow down the reasons and purposes for the practice. But just in case you were drowning in gallons of anointing oil, let me summarize.

Anointing with oil was used to consecrate or set apart someone for special service, like kings or prophets. It was also used in prayers for healing and was a gesture of hospitality and honor toward a guest. Often the words *anointed* and *chosen* are used interchangeably in Scripture.

Psalm 23:5 says God anoints your head with oil. So with those applications of anointing oil in mind, think about the following and journal your responses.

How has my Shepherd King set me apart or consecrated me?

How has my Shepherd King's presence or touch brought healing—emotionally, physically, relationally, or financially?

How have I experienced my Shepherd King's kindness, hospitality, or blessing?

Oil itself is mentioned more than two hundred times in the Bible. And most often when it's used for anointing, it can be applied as a metaphor for the Holy Spirit's presence and action in someone's life. Here's a perfect example—1 Samuel 16:13. What happened when David was anointed with oil?

When Samuel anointed David, that act indicated David was chosen and set apart for special service. In that moment the Spirit of the Lord, or the Holy Spirit, came upon him. So it's not a big stretch to see the anointing of oil in Psalm 23:5 as a poetic picture of the sweet presence and action of the Holy Spirit in our lives.

OK, put down your pen and just sit back and sip your coffee while I tell you a couple of interesting facts about ancient practices of anointing with oil. As you read, pay attention to how this applies to your life.

First, it was custom to honor guests at your table by anointing them with oil. Olive oil was mixed with sweet, fragrant spices. When guests visited someone's home, it was hospitable to wash their feet and place oil on their heads. The longer the dinner lasted, the more oil would trickle down over their hair, cheeks, and neck, cooling the guests and releasing a pleasant fragrance.

Second interesting fact: The practice of anointing was used by shepherds. Lice and other pests would attach their pesky selves into the sheep's wool. If those gross little critters got near the sheep's head it was not only super annoying to the sheep, it could be downright dangerous. If the pests burrowed into the sheep's ears, it could kill them. Awful, isn't it?

So good shepherds would pour oil on the sheep's head to make their wool slippery, creating an insect slip and slide to protect the sheep. In other words, the shepherd anointed the sheep's head with oil to prevent distraction and destruction.[2]

> Combining these ancient practices with what you learned from Scripture about anointing with oil and the Holy Spirit metaphor, how would you now explain what it means for you to be anointed with oil by your Shepherd King?

Sister, when God anoints your head with oil, He is honoring you with the bounty of His blessing. He is overflowing your life with the fullness of His Spirit. He is reminding you once again that He chose you, He protects you, and He calls you His own—you belong to your Shepherd King.

> Read Romans 8:9 and Ephesians 1:13-14, and describe how Scripture explains our relationship with the Holy Spirit.

We receive the Holy Spirit when we receive Christ. He doesn't ever leave us. He seals us. But since we come to the table every day, we can also receive a fresh filling of God's Holy Spirit—the fresh oil of anointing—every day. That doesn't mean you re-receive the Holy Spirit every day. It means you get a renewed awareness of His presence and power to lead you, to strengthen you to obey, and to accomplish God's will. Here's a good way to think about it.

Find Lamentations 3:22-23. What does Jeremiah acknowledge about God's mercies and compassion?

They are "new every morning." Oh thank You, Lord, for that! Is Jeremiah thanking God for new mercies every morning because God had removed His mercies and compassion the night before? No.

Jeremiah is not saying that we lose God's mercy or compassion. They don't disappear from our lives. But rather, every day we get to experience God's mercies all over again, fresh and new. That's what it's like to be anointed with the oil of the Holy Spirit every day. We don't lose the Holy Spirit.

The more we stay in the presence of the Lord, sitting at the table He prepares for us, the more we are aware of the presence and power of His Holy Spirit in our lives.

Finish up today by thanking God for His anointing. And if it's been a while since you've experienced the presence and action of the Holy Spirit in your life, ask God for a fresh "anointing" because that's why God prepares this table for you—so you will be filled to overflowing!

DAY 4

MY CUP RUNS OVER

Hey, hey, hey! Here we are near the end of this verse and this week of study. And all this honor and blessing and joy and celebration at the table is so much you just can't contain it. Your cup is filled to overflowing!

It's interesting that the Scripture doesn't say, "You prepare a table before me in the presence of my enemies; You anoint my head with oil; my cup is half full." Or, "You prepare a table before me in the presence of my enemies; You anoint my head with oil; my cup is half empty."

> If you had to pick, which one of those Scripture misquotes best represents you and why?
>
> Half full:
>
> Half empty:

Oh girl, none of us are all one or the other. We all have our half-full and our half-empty days. However, we do have tendencies toward one or the other. When stress is dogging me, when I'm tired, when there's conflict between me and my husband, Phil, I easily become a half-empty kind of girl. Yep, without the Holy Spirit, my Eeyore tendency wins out.

Here's why I tell you that. You may watch the teaching videos for this study and think I'm a natural half-full optimist all the time. Nope. Actually, I'm a supernatural optimist because of table time with my Shepherd. What I am learning from this verse is that half-full or half-empty don't exist. Sister, not optimism or pessimism—just abundance!

Our cups are overflowing!

> Find in a dictionary or thesaurus some synonyms for *abundance* and *overflow*. List them below.

I found words like *brim over, bubble over, run over, spill over.* Did you notice all the "overs"?

To overflow means you have plenty—more than you can contain. Life is abundant. And that is your Shepherd's intention for you, whether you're in a green pasture, beside still waters, or trudging through a dark valley.

So let's turn this poetry into the practical so we will really know what this kind of abundance and overflow looks like. Carefully read the following six Scripture verses to discern how we are filled and what we will overflow with. (Notice words like *abound* and *filled* also.)

Now may the God of hope fill you with all joy and peace as you believe
so that you may overflow with hope by the power of the Holy Spirit.
ROMANS 15:13, CSB

My cup overflows with:

Scripture tells us God fills us with joy and peace, and then we overflow with hope. Does that describe your life? Explain.

If you're low on hope, how can you get more joy and peace poured into your life?

All this is for your benefit, so that the grace that is reaching more and
more people may cause thanksgiving to overflow to the glory of God.
2 CORINTHIANS 4:15, NIV

My cup overflows with:

Scripture teaches us that grace causes thanksgiving to overflow. Does that describe your life? Why or why not?

Are you receiving the grace God gives you? Explain.

If you want to overflow with thanksgiving, ask God to fill you with His grace.

I am very frank with you; I have great pride in you. I am filled with
encouragement; I am overflowing with joy in all our afflictions.
2 CORINTHIANS 7:4, CSB

My cup overflows with:

Scripture shows that when we are filled with comfort and
encouragement, we will overflow with joy. Does that describe your
life? Why or why not?

Do you need more joy? Explain.

How does this verse teach us that we can receive more joy?

Ask God to comfort and encourage you so you will overflow with joy.

... that your rejoicing for me may be more abundant
in Jesus Christ by my coming to you again.
PHILIPPIANS 1:26

My cup overflows with:

Scripture assures us that when we are filled with Christ, rejoicing overflows. Does that describe your life? Why or why not?

Sometimes grumbling or resentment overflows instead of rejoicing. So, if you need to amp up the rejoicing, how does this verse show you it can happen?

If you want to brim over with rejoicing, pull your chair up to the table and ask God to anoint you with His Spirit.

And may the Lord cause you to increase and overflow with love
for one another and for everyone, just as we do for you.
1 THESSALONIANS 3:12, CSB

My cup overflows with:

Scripture teaches us that God causes us to overflow with love. Does this describe you? Why or why not?

If love isn't oozing out of you, how can that change?

Love isn't always natural, but it is always supernatural. Ask God to cause you to overflow with His love.

> May my lips overflow with praise, for you teach me your decrees.
> PSALM 119:171, NIV

My cup overflows with:

Scripture shows us that being filled with God's Word makes us overflow with praise. Does this describe you? Why or why not?

If you want to overflow with praise, based on this verse, what can you do so you will overflow?

Oh my friend, when we're at the table God prepares for us, God fills us to overflowing. According to Scripture, we will overflow with love, joy, thanksgiving, hope, rejoicing, and praise. We'll have plenty of those things, in abundance.

So look at your life. Do those words characterize you? When you're jostled, do those qualities and responses spill out? When your plans get turned upside down, when you get knocked down, when you start to shake, what brims over from your cup? Only what is inside will flow out.

Take some time with your Shepherd King to think and pray about this. Are you satisfied with what flows from your life?

I overflow with:

I am filled with:

I overflow with:

I am filled with:

I overflow with:

I am filled with:

The Hebrew word for *overflow* in Psalm 23:5 means *saturated*. And it denotes wealth or satisfaction.[3] So, when we are saturated with the good things of God, we will be rich with His Spirit and truth and fully, deeply satisfied. We will be women who lack nothing.

That's the picture God is drawing for us. It's like He's saying, *What I want to give you is bigger than you can contain. What I want to lavish over your life is more than you have capacity to hold. I want to fill you with grace and peace and joy and My Word so you will overflow with hope and love and rejoicing. When I saturate your life with My goodness, you will be satisfied.*

> Take some time to just sit with your Shepherd. Get a cup of coffee or hot tea and just sit at your table with Him. As you sip from your cup, think about the blessings God has filled your life with. Read Malachi 3:10; John 10:10; and Ephesians 3:20-21 to remind you of God's method of blessing your life.

Thank your Shepherd for His overflow of goodness in your life.

> Draw the shape of a coffee mug or tea cup, and then write all over it the blessings you have received from your Shepherd. I bet you will have so many they will overflow the design of your cup. Draw a big one!
>
> Use the following Scriptures to prompt your design: Genesis 27:28-29; 2 Samuel 22:3-4; Psalm 138:7; Isaiah 41:10; John 1:16; Philippians 4:19; James 1:17.

Let's encourage one another as we thank our Shepherd for His goodness. Take a picture of something that represents the blessings that fill your cup to overflowing and share it on Twitter, Facebook, or Instagram. Be sure to use the hashtag #Psalm23Study and include your thanks to God for His blessings in your post. I can't wait to see what you share!

Sister, you can drink from that cup of blessing every day! The Aramaic Bible in plain English translates this phrase, "My cup overflows as if it were alive."[4] I love it! It is as if the cup is vibrating with anticipation, opening wide to contain all that is poured into it!

So hold out and up the cup of your life, and ask God to keep filling you up.

Friend, don't settle for less than all God wants to give you. God has prepared a table before you, and He has made you safe here, in front of your enemies. You can have confidence because He has anointed you. Don't bring a teeny weeny Dixie® cup to the table God prepares for you. Bring a venti size, giant Big Gulp® cup, and lift it up to your Shepherd King. Ask Him to fill it with the blessings of His table and the fullness of His Spirit. He has brought you this far, so drink in His goodness to you and *paaarrrtttttyyy*!

Well girl, verse 5 is a wrap!

This verse really convicts me to enjoy my Shepherd more, to receive His blessing without reservation, and to anticipate His honor and gracious ministry in my life. I am so glad we are learning this together. And I'm so glad that someday you and I will be sitting at a table together at the marriage supper of the Lamb (Rev. 19:6-9). I'm quite certain there will be cloth napkins and coffee. Yes!

Lord, may we feast on the abundance of Your house. May we drink our fill of the river of Your delights. Amen (Ps. 36:8).

Enjoy your Green Pasture Day tomorrow—may God's Spirit keep guiding you into truth.

DAY 5

GREEN PASTURE DAY: A DAY TO REST AND DIGEST

You prepare a table before me in the presence of my enemies;

You anoint my head with oil; my cup runs over.

PSALM 23:5

As you use this day to do whatever helps you digest what you've learned this week, consider that Psalm 23:5 helps us understand the Protection Principle: **You experience confidence and comfort because of your Shepherd's care.**

On your Green Pasture Day, as you rest, pray, journal, draw, worship, or ponder, here are some things to consider:

Scriptures I want to remember from this week:

Quotes I liked from this week:

Provision, Protection, Presence, and Pleasure Sightings from this week:

There are some really great songs that help us RSVP and enjoy table times with the Lord. Check out my *Psalm 23* playlist for verse 5 at JenniferRothschild.com/Psalm23, and use it to fill your cup!

Thank You, Lord, for setting the table just for me and filling my life with blessing.

GROUP SESSION 6

Welcome and Prayer

VIDEO NOTES

In Hebrew *lo* is a negation meaning "_____."

Debar can be translated as "_____" or "_____." *Debar* means
"_____ of _____."

Two Things That Will Occur at Our King's Table

1. _____

2. _____

Our Shepherd King saves a seat for us at the table, and He says, "_____
_____!"

God prepares a place for us at His table. And He chooses to _____ with us
and _____ us for Jesus' sake.

The Hebrew meaning for *anointed* is "to be _____ _____."

When the King's table was being served, there was never an _____ cup.

Many of us need to learn to _____ _____ all that God wants to
give us.

The Hebrew meaning of *overflow* is "_____."

Everything your Shepherd wants to give you, you then can have the opportunity to give
to _____.

CONVERSATION GUIDE
Video 6

DAY 1: What are some of your favorite table time experiences with friends and family?
What made them so special?
How do you see God's "table" evident in your life?
Share some of the "sightings" (provision, protection, presence, pleasure) you
experienced this week.

DAY 2: Do you ever peg people as your enemies, losing sight of who the real enemy is?
Explain.
How does the enemy attack you? Where are you most vulnerable to his attacks?
How have you seen the Lord work powerfully to give you victory over the enemy?

DAY 3: How has the Shepherd King set you apart and consecrated you?
Where have you seen the Holy Spirit's work in your life?

DAY 4: How is God causing your cup to overflow with love, joy, and thanksgiving? And
how are you seeing that splash over onto the people you interact with?

DAY 5: Share some of the highlights from your Green Pasture Day.
What is one significant truth you take away from this week of study?

Do you need to be reminded of what you just heard? Get my written
summary of this video teaching at jenniferrothschild.com/Psalm23.

WEEK 6

YOUR SHEPHERD
BRINGS YOU HOME

Surely goodness and mercy shall follow me all the days of my life; and I will dwell in the house of the LORD forever.

PSALM 23:6

#PSALM23STUDY

Hey, girl. I'll start with a confession. There are few things more satisfying to me than to be smack-dab in the middle of reading a great book. There are also few things more disappointing to me than to be in the last chapter of a great book. I will slow down just to make it last longer because I never want a good book to end. That's exactly how I feel about studying Psalm 23 with you. I don't want it to end!

This is the final verse of Psalm 23 (insert deep sigh of regret here). David has come to this conclusion after journeying through the green pastures, down the path of righteousness, through dark valleys, and into the banquet hall of God. He looks back at his life while at the same time looking forward. He affirms that God's goodness and mercy have followed and will continue to follow him all his days. And this week, that's what we'll do too! But let's try to slow down and make it last as long as possible, OK?

We'll look at specific words and phrases in this verse to help us understand the depth of this promise.

WORD 1: SURELY

How many times have you heard this verse, or another verse or sentence that begins with "surely," quoted and some wannabe comedian jumps in with, "Don't call me Shirley!"? Oh, brother. That right there is my husband. He thinks it's funny every time. Not me. I didn't even think it was funny the first time. But, *surely* is a little word that can have a big impact on the way we live, so I don't want us to speed past it.

Surely, in the original Hebrew, is what is called an adverbial particle. I know that sounds like something you should vacuum up from your carpet! However, in Hebrew, that part of speech denotes a very strong, positive assertion of truth. The Hebrew word for *surely* also is translated as *certainly, completely,* and *only*. Those are some hefty, emphatic words aren't they? They don't leave much doubt that what follows them is the unbending, unalterable, non-negotiable truth.

When David looked back at his life and forward to his future, he settled on the truth that only two things had followed him and would follow him. He was certain it was completely true that only goodness and mercy followed him.

Really? Only goodness and mercy followed him? Only?

Think about what you know about David's life. What else could have followed him?

Peruse 2 Samuel 11:1–12:23. From this story, we see that David could easily have had a long train of guilt and shame following him all the days of his life. List the reasons why and the verse(s) that affirm those reasons in the space provided.

REASONS FOR GUILT AND SHAME

REFERENCE	REASON

The guilt, shame, and pain of David's affair with Bathsheba, the murder of her husband, and the death of their baby could have plagued him all his life. Remember, David likely wrote this psalm as an older man after living many seasons. So certainly the Israeli gossip magazines never forgot his sins and mistakes and likely rehashed them after every victory or defeat.

But the same David who had such a résumé of shame was the same David who wrote that *only* goodness and mercy would follow him. How could he say that with his sinful track record? Is it because he took his sin so lightly? Or maybe he just presumed upon the grace of God? What do you think?

The key to David's statement in verse 6 of Psalm 23 is perhaps found in his plea from Psalm 51.

Read Psalm 51, keeping in mind that this was David's response after being confronted about his sin with Bathsheba. As you read the psalm, make a list of the direct requests David made to God. (Hint, hint—look for the words "me" and "my" to get started. I found fourteen.)

Psalm 51 Requests:

David confessed, repented, and asked for God's cleansing and restoration. Based on 1 John 1:9, how did God respond to David's request?

David confessed. God cleansed.

When David looked back at his life, he didn't see his sin; he saw God's mercy. When he looked behind him, he didn't see his shame—he saw God's goodness. God blotted out his sin and created in him "a clean heart" (Ps. 51:10). His Shepherd restored to him the joy of his salvation. The Lord renewed a right spirit in him and delivered him from guilt.

Where there was guilt, there is now only goodness.

Where there were mistakes, there is now only mercy.

Look again at the list you made from Psalm 51. Grab a permanent marker, and write one of the following words over each of David's requests: *goodness, mercy, cleansed,* or *forgiven*. You can choose whichever word you want and, of course, feel free to repeat them over and over! Pause and examine how God's goodness and mercy covered all the sin and guilt of David's past—and now covers yours.

When you look at your life, what follows you? Do you see well-worn trails of goodness and mercy like David did? Or only the dusty reminders of guilt and shame? Explain.

Remember Charlie Brown's hygiene-challenged buddy, Pig-Pen? He was known for his perpetually filthy overalls and that cloud of dirt and dust that followed him everywhere he went. No matter how the little Peanut tried, he just couldn't seem to shake off that fog of grunge—it followed him all the days of his life!

Well, like Pig-Pen, a cloud of dirt can easily follow us if we let it. But sister, that doesn't have to be our story. Consider your life. Is there a perpetual haze of shame and guilt surrounding you, following you? Pause here with your Shepherd and pray about this.

I'll give you some prayer or journal prompts, and then use a separate journal or the space provided here to get honest with your Shepherd.

The shame that follows me is …

The guilt I can't seem to shake is due to …

The sin I haven't confessed is …

The sin God has forgiven me for but I can't forgive myself for is …

The mistake that weighs me down is ...

Goodness and mercy are supposed to follow us, not shame and guilt. Only goodness and mercy. Your past sin doesn't have to tag along. Leave it nailed to the cross of Christ and buried under the grace of Jesus.

Review your responses, and then reread your Psalm 51 request list one more time to remind you of your Shepherd's intention for you—forgiveness, cleansing, goodness, and mercy. If you journaled your prayer responses, take out that permanent marker again, and write over your responses with *goodness, mercy, cleansed,* or *forgiven.* Take some time with your Shepherd. Don't move forward until you have received His forgiveness, restoration, or assurance.

OK, *honesty alert*! I agree with this truth—I celebrate it and trust it. I know I'm forgiven. I know I'm clean. I know I'm loved. I know He has been good and merciful to me.

And then tomorrow morning when I wake up, wham! Guilt and mistakes wake up in me, revved up and ready for another day of following me around. The sin that God has forgotten, I remember. The guilt that God removed, I try to retrieve! Does this happen to you?

So how do we really do this, not just on the page of a Bible study, but in our real, imperfect lives? How do we kick guilt and shame to the curb so only goodness and mercy follow us?

First, we always follow Scripture and respond like David did. There is no substitute. If it's guilt over sin, repent. If it's shame, rebuke it! Keep the truth of Scripture always before you. Here are a few verses to keep you moving forward.

Read the following passages, and write the truth you can stand on.

2 Corinthians 5:17

Galatians 2:20

Philippians 3:13-14

1 John 1:9

Hebrews 12:1-2

Sister, there is no formula; there is only faith. So lean hard on your Shepherd and trust His voice.

And if you're like me and you like to see it in everyday vernacular, I'll let you in on an über-practical thing I do. Now, I may be blind but I think in pictures. So here is the picture I imagine that helps me see this truth.

I imagine that when I wake up in the morning, goodness and mercy are waiting at my bedroom door to follow me out of my room and into my day. I think of them like anxious sheepdogs, panting with excitement and ready to follow me, an easily-rattled sheep, nudging me forward. It's like I can't get out the door without them on my heels.

Even if you don't want goodness and mercy to tag along, too bad! You will stumble over them to get out of the door—they will be on your heels whether you like it or not!

Try it! If you notice some shame or guilt trying to reattach to you, stop. I mean, literally, if you are walking, stop and speak the truth out loud: "Only, as in o-n-l-y, goodness and mercy will follow me today!" I've done it, and sister, I'll keep doing it!

I pray your time with your Shepherd today was comforting, affirming, and liberating, too, because He is always leading you down the path of righteousness.

Let's finish up today by just resting in God's Word.

> Read Psalm 103, and meditate on God's compassion, forgiveness, mercy, and love for you.

What about you? What's something super-practical that you do to kick guilt and shame to the curb so only goodness and mercy follow you? Let's learn from each other. Share with your Bible study buddies and ask what they do too. And you can even share it on social media—be sure to use the hashtag #Psalm23Study.

Tomorrow, we will focus on what exactly this goodness and mercy is, and you will be so encouraged!

Until then, "Never let loyalty and faithfulness leave you. Tie them around your neck; write them on the tablet of your heart" (Prov. 3:3, CSB).

DAY 2

Well, I hope you experienced *only* goodness and mercy following you yesterday. There is so much and so much more in this verse. Today, we'll look at three more words in verse 6, starting with *goodness*.

WORD 2: GOODNESS

Find the English dictionary definition for *goodness* and jot it down:

Goodness means *that which is pleasing, valuable* or *useful.* And in the original Hebrew, *goodness* means *a good thing, benefit,* or *welfare.*

Complete the phrase below without using the word *goodness*. Instead, use words from the English and Hebrew definitions.
"[Only] _____ and mercy shall follow me all the days of my life."

David is saying that only what is valuable, pleasing, useful, beneficial, and for our good will follow us all the days of our lives. Hmmm—ponder that for a moment.

Has every experience in your life been good, beneficial, or useful?

Think of a situation or circumstance from your past that didn't seem all that good at the time. What was it?

What were your thoughts and emotions during that experience?

Did you receive any value or benefit from that not-so-good situation or circumstance while you were in the middle of it? Explain.

Have you received anything beneficial or useful over time? If so, what?

Now pause and hold those thoughts.

WORD 3: MERCY

Mercy means *compassion, a disposition to be kind and forgiving,* and *showing great kindness.*

In Hebrew, *mercy* can be described as *loving-kindness.*

So write the phrase again, using words from the definitions of *mercy* to finish the phrase:

"[Only] _____ and _____ shall follow me all the days of my life."

Hmmm—ponder that for a moment.

Has every experience in your life so far been full of kindness, compassion, forgiveness, or love?

Think of a past situation or circumstance that was not characterized by loving-kindness at the time. What was it?

What were your thoughts and emotions during that experience?

Have you experienced any deeper understanding of compassion or loving-kindness now that the harsh, unkind, or merciless circumstance is in your past? If so, how?

OK, let's pause for a bit and consider how it's all goodness and mercy following us when what we experience is not always good. Pour some coffee or tea.

Do you or the people in your world ever say the phrase, "It's all good"? For instance, if somebody stumbles, face plants on the sidewalk, and you ask, "Are you OK?" They say, "It's all good!" Clearly, it's not so good when they have a bloody nose and bruised pride, but they still say, "It's all good." Why do you think they do that?

Oh girl, there are lots of unsearchable reasons we humans use that phrase. But I think it's a spoken desire for the hopeful future outcome rather than the present reality. We desperately want to believe it is all good, that everything will end up working together for good even if it isn't inherently good at the moment.

Let's build a biblical case for this thought. We'll use the apostle Paul as our case study.

Read 2 Corinthians 11:24-27, and describe Paul's not-so-good experiences.

Read Philippians 1:12-14, and describe the good that came from Paul's not-so-good.

Read Romans 8:28, and describe Paul's conclusion as to why all the not-so-good is still good.

Pause from your case-building for a clarification. The most accurate rendering of this verse is "God works all things for good," not, "all things work themselves together for good." Our Shepherd is the One who uses it all for good—our good, the good of others, and for His good purposes.

Read Philippians 2:13 to affirm this truth.

OK, almost done. Find Romans 8:35-39, and describe why only goodness and mercy will follow us.

Nothing separates you from the goodness and mercy of your Shepherd. Even the not-so-good in His Hands becomes only good. You can look at your life through the lens of "only goodness and mercy," and that perspective changes how you see your life circumstances.

So what is your conclusion to your case study? Since goodness and mercy are emphatic and non-negotiable, following you in every situation and every season, what does that say about your not-so-good situations and seasons?

Maybe we all need to say, "It's all good!" a little more for all the right reasons, huh?

It is all good because of our good Shepherd. Wow, I need to pause and praise right here. The Lord is our Shepherd, we truly lack nothing. OK, sister, we're not done yet. One more Hebrew word before we close.

WORD 4: FOLLOW

This word for *follow* is a very specific Hebrew word. If we don't understand the true meaning of this word, we may misunderstand God's action toward us. We might think *follow* means *trail behind and never quite catch up,* kind of like a teenager who doesn't want to be seen with mom at the mall. If God's goodness and mercy followed us that way, it wouldn't be very comforting or encouraging, would it? You would have to rewrite the verse, "Surely goodness and mercy will lag behind me and never quite catch up all the days of my life."

Fortunately, that's *not* the true meaning of the word. The Hebrew word for *follow* is *râdaph* which means *to pursue, chase,* and *attend closely upon.*

> So write out the verse one more time replacing the word *follow* with the Hebrew definitions. (Include the definitions for *goodness* and *mercy* you already used.)
>
> "[Only] _____ and _____ shall
>
> _____ me all the days of my life."

Girl, God pursues us and chases us down with goodness and mercy every single day of our lives! Let me illustrate what this looks like.

I get to see a picture of it every day with my little diva dog, Lucy. Come in the kitchen with me, and I'll show you. Around noon I grab a piece of string cheese from the fridge, close the door, and usually open that little mozzarella tube right there so I can throw away the wrapper. As soon as Lucy hears the vacuum seal broken and the wrapper being removed, she's right there on my heels. I usually grab some crackers from the pantry, trying not to trip over her, then head to my kitchen table with the cheese still in my hand and a paper plate tucked under my arm. (Classy, I know.)

If I stop walking suddenly, her little wet nose jams into my calf. I can't take a step that she doesn't match, right behind me, not inching back one bit until that cheese is gone. She is following me in constant, dedicated pursuit! Girl, if I've got cheese, I've got Lucy pursuing me—all the days of my life.

In similar fashion, the Shepherd's goodness and mercy pursue you. **God is forever with you and for you. He chases you with His loving-kindness and goodness.** Do you need to stop dead in your tracks so you can feel goodness and mercy bump into you? Sometimes we run so fast trying to escape our problems or outrun our shame that we don't slow down enough to receive and experience the goodness and mercy we need most.

God's goodness isn't just His response to our guilt. It's His remedy for our discouragement. We can be encouraged that He will take all the not-so-good and work it for good. Oh my friend, when you let goodness and mercy catch you, you experience Romans 8:28. It's all good.

We know that all things work together for the good of those who love God, who are called according to His purpose.

ROMANS 8:28, CSB

Even though all our Hebrew and English definitions describe what goodness and mercy are, those words also describe who God is. He is good. He is merciful. And He is your Shepherd. Take some time with the definitions of *goodness* and *mercy* in mind to praise and thank your Shepherd for who He is and who He is to you.

Oh my friend, God doesn't just give you mercy. He is mercy.

He doesn't just respond with goodness. He is goodness.

You can't outrun His goodness to you. You can't sprint fast enough that mercy, His loving-kindness, won't overtake you. So slow down and receive it.

OK, my sister, see ya tomorrow!

Using Scripture to pray and praise helps me keep focused. I meditated on Exodus 33:19 and 34:6 as I was writing this section of the study. Use this space to list any Scripture the Lord brings to mind as you pause to thank God for who He is.

DAY 3

ALL THE DAYS OF MY LIFE

"Like sands through the hourglass—so are the days of our lives!"[1] (Cue cheesy soap opera music.) I couldn't resist! When I was in college, my roommate designed her entire class schedule around that soap opera. She didn't want to miss an episode. And, my sweet Granny called *Days of Our Lives*, along with *General Hospital*, her "stories." She had to watch her stories everyday while she ate a MoonPie® and sipped on an RC Cola®! You didn't mess with Mama when her "stories" were on! (Can you tell she was just a tad Southern?)

Psalm 23 is a story. Your story. The story of you and your Shepherd—all the days of your life. So think about this psalm as a series of episodes. The writers of one of my Granny's soap operas would have created a storyboard for each episode. A storyboard is a graphic depiction of how the episode unfolds—shot by shot. It's made up of a series of illustrations along with notes or dialogue to show what is going on in the scene, kind of like a comic strip with several scenes.

So I want you to draw your own storyboard of this psalm. Even if you have little or no artistic ability and have to use stick figures, draw inside the series of boxes below to illustrate each scene of the psalm.

VERSE 1

VERSE 2

VERSE 3

VERSE 4

VERSE 5

What do you notice about where your Shepherd is in the first few scenes? Where are you? Where does He seem to be in verse 6?

What does this show you about where you are and where God is?

Every scene, every single day of your life, God is with you—before you, beside you, and behind you. The Shepherd is with you. Beautiful, isn't it? (I'm talking about the truth being beautiful, not necessarily your artwork! Ha!)

Now, let's write a script of sorts for your storyboard. This will be your own personal story. Use the verses below along with all six verses of Psalm 23 to communicate the narrative of Psalm 23. Rephrase the verses into first person, you talking about or to your Shepherd. (I gave you mine as an example.)

SCRIPT/STORY STARTERS:

VERSE 1: Combine Psalm 23:1 with Nahum 1:7

VERSE 2: Combine Psalm 23:2 with Psalm 16:8

VERSE 3: Combine Psalm 23:3 with Jeremiah 6:16a

VERSE 4: Combine Psalm 23:4 with Isaiah 58:8 and Psalm 5:12

VERSE 5: Combine Psalm 23:5 with Psalm 3:3

VERSE 6: Combine Psalm 23:6 with Psalm 125:2

HERE'S MY SCRIPT/STORY:

VERSE 1: The Lord, my Shepherd, is so good. There is nothing I lack because He is a refuge for me all the time, but especially in times of trouble.

VERSE 2: He cares for me as I trust in Him. I keep my eyes on Him; He is always before me, leading me to green pastures and still waters. He stays beside me, and that's why I won't get shaken up by life.

VERSE 3: When I stand at the crossroads, not sure of the path, God shows me the path. I walk in it and find rest for my soul.

VERSE 4: Even when life is dark, the Lord blesses me. He surrounds me with His favor, and His glory is guarding me. He's got my back. I am comforted and not afraid.

VERSE 5: When I am before my enemies, my Shepherd blesses me and protects me like a shield around me. I don't need to hang my head in shame because He lifts my head high.

VERSE 6: And finally, as the mountains surround Jerusalem, God, my Shepherd, surrounds me, and He has surrounded me now and forevermore. I will dwell in His house forever.

No matter what the specific details your own personal storyboard may include, the truths of this Scripture script remain and represent the ultimate truth of your story. Your Shepherd is beside you, behind you, before you, for you, and with you all the days of your life.

You may want to take a picture or make a copy of your story and put it in a place you will see it often. This will help remind you of your Shepherd's goodness, mercy, and His constant care.

I figured weaving Scriptures to create a script may have taken a little more time, so that's all we're going to do today. Finish up your time with your Shepherd by reviewing each scene of your story. You may want to look back through the book and review the quotes and verses you wrote down on your Green Pasture Days to help put yourself back inside each verse, each scene. Just linger with your Shepherd, and ask His Holy Spirit to remind you of truth.

Girl, do you realize goodness and mercy invade every scene of your story? You are being chased by goodness and mercy all the days of your life, all the way to the house of the Lord. Tomorrow we'll run to His house, but today run to His heart—to Him. Let His goodness and mercy spur you on.

Thank You, Lord, that in every scene of our stories You are right there, the main character. Help us to clearly recognize Your presence all the days of our lives. Amen.

DAY 4

AND I WILL DWELL IN THE HOUSE OF THE LORD FOREVER

Well, this is the last day we will spend together, my friend. I've got my coffee. I'm sitting at my same glass kitchen table where we started this thing, and I'm thinking of how much I love this psalm, how much I love the Shepherd of this psalm, and how much I love you, my sheep sister! We are in this flock together. We will finish up in the house of the Lord today. Not a bad place to end, huh?

Open your Bible and reread the whole psalm again. This last verse of Psalm 23 says we "will dwell in the house of the LORD forever" (v. 6). *Forever.* So before we really examine how dwelling in the house of the Lord impacts our futures, let's think about how dwelling in the house of the Lord influences our here and now.

> What do you think of when you hear the words "house of the LORD forever"?

You may have thought of words like *eternal* or *everlasting*. But I bet, I hope, you thought of one of my favorite words: *heaven*.

> Do you ever dwell on heaven? Do you think about it much? Should you?

Let's see how much Scripture dwells on heaven to help inform how much we should. Do a word search or topical search on *heaven*, and compile biblical reasons why thinking about heaven is beneficial, encouraging, and important. I've included some Scripture starters to get you going.

REFERENCE	WHY THINK ABOUT HEAVEN?
Isaiah 25:8-12	
Jeremiah 50:5	
John 14:2-4	
Philippians 3:20	
Colossians 3:2	
Revelation 22:1-5	

Dwelling on heaven helps us anticipate dwelling in heaven! Heaven is our home—the place Jesus prepares for us where there are no tears, no curse, and no night. Heaven is the place of our true citizenship, the place where we can look into our Shepherd's face and serve Him forever. It is our hope and our reality. And sister, there are some days that dwelling on heaven is what keeps me going. It helps my perspective.

I've already been honest with you about my blindness, so I'm sure it's no surprise to you that there are some days when I fight discouragement. It's those days I focus on heaven.

My friend, I know you have those days too. The difficulties, the grief, the injustice of life here can become so heavy. Perhaps on those days you also need to turn your thoughts to heaven. Remember this earth is not your final destination. Earthly life is short, but heavenly life is long. The same goodness and mercy that pursue us also propel us toward our heavenly home. So even now, we can set our minds on heaven and the things of heaven. When we do, the earth issues that feel so big become right-sized in light of eternity.

Setting your mind on your ultimate home will encourage you when your valley is dark or your path is rocky.

A practical way I do this is by reading Scriptures about heaven, like 1 Thessalonians 4:16-18. (Because of the previous exercise you have your own heaven Scripture list too!) And I created my own heaven playlist. (You can find it at JenniferRothschild.com/Psalm23.)

But is heaven the same thing as "the house of the LORD" here in Psalm 23:6? Is David talking specifically about our eternal home? To find out, we need to understand what Scripture means by "the house of the LORD"

Find some other verses where *house of the LORD* shows up. (You may also want to search for *house of God* and *the Lord's house* or *dwelling place*.) I've included some Scriptures to get you started.

Psalm 15:1-2 • Psalm 84 • Psalm 122:1 • Ecclesiastes 5:1
Luke 2:49 • 1 Corinthians 3:16 • _____
_____ • _____ • _____

How do the verses listed answer the following questions?
What is the house of the Lord?

Where is it?

How do you get in?

Who is allowed there?

Is it a building?

You probably found a variety of verses that were more confusing than clarifying about what exactly the house of the Lord is! That's understandable since there are so many different contexts for these references. Some verses point to a physical space like the tabernacle or temple. Some verses give the impression that maybe it's not just a physical place. Maybe it is heaven. And the New Testament tells us that we, ourselves, when we are born again are the temple of the Holy Spirit!

But all these different references do have something in common. Think about what it is, and jot down your thoughts.

What makes the house of the Lord or temple or tabernacle or any other location a dwelling place of the Lord is God Himself—His presence. God's presence is holy and full of glory, so that makes the place He dwells full of glory. Some of the verses suggest that no one can approach or dwell in the house of the Lord without purity and humility. Every reference makes it clear that God reigns and that He is to be honored in His house.

When we boil it down, to "dwell in the house of the LORD" means to be in God's presence. And there is nothing and nowhere more satisfying than being in His house. Sounds a lot like heaven, too, doesn't it?

It seems, sister, that we cannot only dwell on, but we can dwell in the God's house right here, right now, as we abide with our Shepherd.

Read Psalm 27:4. What was David's request?

Do you have the same request? Explain.

Read this verse several times and meditate on it. Pray it to the Lord. Then, think about or journal the following.

How am I dwelling in the house of the Lord right now?

How am I gazing on the beauty of the Lord right now?

How am I seeking Him in His temple right now?

If you're not satisfied with your answers, what changes do you need to make?

Pray for grace and ask a Bible study buddy to help you with this.

Sister, you may be in your kitchen or at your desk. You may be in an airport or in your backyard. But if you sincerely ask to "dwell in the house of the LORD" and "gaze on the beauty of the LORD" and "seek him in his temple" (Ps. 27:4, NIV), your Shepherd will answer. No matter where you are right now, you can say with the same confidence as David, "I will dwell in the house of the LORD forever" (23:6) because it is true—your Shepherd is with you.

God invites us to dwell in His house forever. We will dwell with Him in heaven someday. But forever has already started. You are dwelling right now in His house. The whole world is His sanctuary. Every created thing brings Him praise. Wherever God is becomes a sacred place. This planet is full of God's presence.

Now, let's make sure we get this right—that we have a biblical understanding so nobody mistakenly thinks that Jennifer Rothschild suggested we all hug trees and don't bother worshiping at a local church! We do value and steward creation, for it reflects God's character and beauty. And, we do need—and I did say *need*—to gather with believers and worship our Shepherd together often. Yet, experiencing God's presence is not reserved only for a sanctuary on Sunday.

> Look at the following verses to see why right here, right now you are dwelling in the house of the Lord. Draw a big, round planet Earth, and fill it in with words and phrases from the following verses (or other verses you find). These will help you see how you are always in God's presence, that where He is becomes His sanctuary; and consequently, every created thing and your very breath is a praise to Him.

> Psalm 19:1-6 • Psalm 65:4-13 • Isaiah 6:3 • Habakkuk 2:20
> Acts 17:24-25 • _____ • _____
> _____ • _____ • _____

Oh girl, you can dwell in the house of the Lord right here, right now while you are living on planet Earth. Charles Spurgeon said it much better than I can:

> While I am here I will be a child at home with my God; the whole world shall be his house to me; and when I ascend into the upper chamber, I shall not change my company, nor even change the house; I shall only go to dwell in the upper storey of the house of the Lord for ever.[2]
>
> C. H. SPURGEON

Don't you love that? He's just saying, *When I die, I'm going to climb the stairs. I'm not going home; I've been home all along. I just get to experience home from a different room.*

This is why we dwell on heaven before we dwell in heaven. It helps us live the reality of God's presence—the Shepherd with me. If you and I live each day like we are dwelling in the house of the Lord, rather than just longing for it and looking forward to it, we will experience the whole benefit of our Shepherd's presence. Since purity and humility are required to enter into the house of the Lord, let's live pure and humble lives so we don't miss out on the fullness of being with our Shepherd and giving Him the worship He deserves.

Looks like we're at the finish line. Hard to believe, right? There is still so much to learn, so I won't say we're done. I'll just say we have to quit for now. I hope you keep digging and learning with the Holy Spirit as your teacher. This verse may be the last of Psalm 23, but it can be the start of a deeper life, walking with your Shepherd.

Through this psalm, and through your life, He has led you and guided you. He has walked beside you and behind you. He is for you and your very life is from Him. Every step you take, you take with your Shepherd. Everywhere you go, you are drawn by your Shepherd. He provides. He leads. He restores. He protects. He comforts. He blesses. You with the Shepherd and the Shepherd with you. Forever and forever. Amen.

OK, coffee's empty; heart is full! Enjoy your Green Pasture Day tomorrow. See ya, sister!

For an inspiring finish to our study, listen to the Psalm 23 playlist. (Find it at JenniferRothschild.com/Psalm23.) Start with verse 6 songs, and then take a walk, pop in your headphones, and worship right along with all creation.

DAY 5

GREEN PASTURE DAY: A DAY TO REST AND DIGEST

Surely goodness and mercy shall follow me all the days of
my life; and I will dwell in the house of the LORD forever.

PSALM 23:6

As you use this day to digest what you've learned this week, consider that Psalm 23:6 helps us understand the Progress Principle: We are always moved by, moving toward, and moving with our Shepherd.

On your Green Pasture Day, as you rest, pray, journal, draw, worship, or ponder, here are some things to consider:

Scriptures I want to remember from this week:

Quotes I liked from this week:

Thank You, Lord, that I am dwelling in Your house even now and can't ever outrun Your goodness and mercy.

A LAST NOTE FROM ME

Just as I finished up this study, my Hero Dad "climbed the stairs" and went home to heaven. I told you during Week 4 how I feared the loss and grief, and girl, it was hard; it still is. My heart will always ache, but I know heaven will last longer than this grief I feel now. This pain is teaching me once again that I am safe with my Shepherd. He really does care for us and hold us close.

I pray during this study that God drew you close to Himself and you felt His care and companionship also. We really are safe with the Shepherd, and that means we are safe with the sheep. So stay connected with your Bible study buddies. And I'd love to stay connected too. You can find me on all the usual social media channels, and my blog is JenniferRothschild.com. Pop over and sign up for my weekly encouraging email.

And speaking of buddies, I must give a big shout out to mine because, sister, this Bible study just wouldn't have happened without them. Paula Voris, Joan Petty, Denise Alvarez, and my awesome editor, Mike Wakefield—thank you from the bottom of my heart for every single thing!

So let's keep loving each other well and following our Shepherd. Until the next study.

Jennifer

GROUP SESSION 7

BEFORE THE VIDEO

Welcome and Prayer

VIDEO NOTES

In every verse of Psalm 23, we see the _____ of _____.

The Names of God in Psalm 23

Verse 1   The Lord is my shepherd;
          I shall not want.
          Jehovah-Jireh (the Lord, our _____)

Verse 2   He makes me to lie down in green pastures;
          He leads me beside the still waters.
          Jehovah-Shalom (the Lord, my _____)

Verse 3   He restores my soul;
          Jehovah-Rophe (the Lord, my _____)

          He leads me in the paths of righteousness
          For His name's sake.
          Jehovah-Tsidkenu (the Lord, my _____)

Verse 4   Yea, though I walk through the valley of the shadow of death,
          I will fear no evil;
          For You are with me;
          Your rod and Your staff, they comfort me.
          Jehovah-Shama (the Lord is _____.)

Verse 5   You prepare a table before me in the presence of my enemies;
          Jehovah-Nissi (the Lord, our _____)[3]

          You anoint my head with oil;
          My cup runs over.
          Jehovah-Manah (the Lord, our _____)

Verse 6   Surely goodness and mercy shall follow me
         All the days of my life;
         And I will dwell in the house of the LORD
         Forever.
         Jehovah-Cheleq (the LORD, our _____)[4]

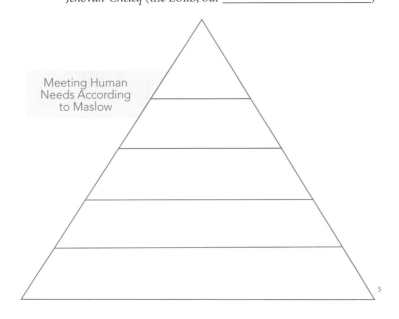

God doesn't just _____ us mercy. He _____ mercy to us.

When we allow ourselves to get "caught" by goodness and mercy, it will change how we _____.

GOODNESS GRABBERS

- _____ is never a bad choice.

- Earth is short. _____ is long.

When we allow ourselves to get "caught" by goodness and mercy, it's going to change what we _____.

When we are in a relationship, we will do one of four things:

1. _____

2. _____

3. _____

4. _____ [6]

"The house of the LORD" is _____ (Ps. 23:6).

DAY 1: What seems to have followed you most of your days, goodness and mercy or shame and guilt? Explain.

How do you keep shame and guilt from being your constant companions?

DAY 2: How have you seen God's goodness in your life in a not-so-good season?

Do you truly believe God works all things for good? Why or why not? How have you seen that already take place in your life or the lives of those around you?

DAY 3: Share the details of your Psalm 23 storyboard.

What conclusions, challenges, or encouragement do you draw from your storyboard?

DAY 4: Do you ever think about heaven? Explain.

What does it mean to dwell in the house of the Lord? How are you presently doing that?

DAY 5: Share some of the highlights from your Green Pasture Day.

What is one significant truth you take away from this week of study?

Do you want to get a summary of my last video teaching?
Go to JenniferRothschild.com/Psalm23.

BIBLE STUDY RESOURCES

There are so many resources available to help us dig deeper into God's Word. It's wonderful, but it can be overwhelming. Where to start? Who to trust? Here are a few tried and true go-to resources you can use during this study:

ONLINE TOOLS

BibleGateway.com
BibleHub.com
BlueLetterBible.org
BibleStudyTools.com
Daily Audio Bible
The Bible App (YouVersion)

PRINT RESOURCES

The New Strong's Expanded Exhaustive Concordance of the Bible by James Strong
Matthew Henry's Concise Commentary on the Whole Bible by Matthew Henry
Holman Bible Commentaries
The New American Commentaries
The Zondervan Encyclopedia of the Bible by Merrill C. Tenney and Moisés Silva
Women of the Word by Jen Wilkin
Rick Warren's Bible Study Methods by Rick Warren

BIBLE STUDY METHODS

As you learn to study the Bible on your own, Stacey Thacker's LIFE method of Bible study is a great starting place. For more information, visit StaceyThacker.com or read her book, *Is Jesus Worth It?*

LEADER HELPS

Thanks so much for leading your group through this study! I know you'll experience much joy and many blessings as you help walk your group through this psalm. I'm praying for you as you take on this responsibility.

Go to JenniferRothschild.com/Psalm23 for a personal prayer and word from me, plus extra resources to enhance your study gatherings.

STUDY FORMAT

GROUP SESSIONS: Each group session contains the following elements: Welcome and Prayer / Watch the Video / Group Discussion. The group discussion provides questions generated from the previous week's personal study and the video teaching. Feel free to adapt, skip, or add questions according to the needs of your group.

PERSONAL STUDY: Each session contains five days of personal study to help participants dig into the Word of God for themselves. The fifth day, the Green Pasture Day, is constructed to be a reflective summary and application of what has been previously studied.

BEING AN EFFECTIVE LEADER

Three keys to being an effective leader of your group:

1. **PREPARE:** Make sure you've watched the teaching video and completed each week's personal study before the group session. Review the discussion questions, and consider how best to lead your group through this time.

2. **PRAY:** Set aside time each week to pray for yourself and for each member of your group. Though organizing and planning are important, protect your time of prayer before each gathering.

3. **CONNECT:** Find ways to interact and stay engaged with the women in your group throughout the study. Make use of social media, email, and handwritten notes to encourage them. Don't stop the connection when the study ends. Continue to encourage and challenge the women in your group in their spiritual journeys.

BONUS FEATURE

Note: the song "Safe in the Arms of Jesus" by Michael O'Brien is included under the Bonus Features on the DVD set of the *Psalm 23* leader kit. Consider using it to open or conclude your group sessions. The song is also available as a free download at JenniferRothschild.com/Psalm23.

ENDNOTES

WEEK 1

1.Chad Brand, Charles Draper, Archie England, eds. *Holman Bible Dictionary* (Nashville: B&H, 2003) accessed via MyWsb.com.

WEEK 2

1. W. Phillip Keller, *A Shepherd Looks at Psalm 23* (Grand Rapids, MI: Zondervan, 1970), 41-42.

WEEK 3

1. "Definition of Restore," *Blue Letter Bible*, https://www.blueletterbible.org/lang/lexicon/lexicon.cfm?Strongs=H7725&t=KJV, accessed May 14, 2018.
2. "Definition of Soul," *Blue Letter Bible,* https://www.blueletterbible.org/lang/lexicon/lexicon.cfm?Strongs=H5315&t=KJV, accessed on May 14, 2018.
3. "Definition of Guide," *Blue Letter Bible,* https://www.blueletterbible.org/lang/lexicon/lexicon.cfm?Strongs=H5148&t=KJV, accessed on May 14, 2018.
4. "Definition of Righteousness," *Blue Letter Bible,* https://www.blueletterbible.org/lang/lexicon/lexicon.cfm?Strongs=H6664&t=KJV, accessed on May 14, 2018.
5. John Piper, "The Shepherd, the Host, and the Highway Patrol," *Desiring God*, September 8, 1980, https://www.desiringgod.org/messages/the-shepherd-the-host-and-the-highway-patrol.

WEEK 4

1. *HCSB Study Bible* (Nashville: Holman Bible Publishers, 2010), 903.
2. "Definition of Shadow of Death, *Blue Letter Bible,* https://www.blueletterbible.org/lang/lexicon/lexicon.cfm?Strongs=H6757&t=KJV, accessed on May 30, 2018.
3. "Definition of Death," *Blue Letter Bible*, https://www.blueletterbible.org/lang/lexicon/lexicon.cfm?Strongs=H4194, accessed on May 30, 2018.
4. "Definition of Rod," *Blue Letter Bible*, https://www.blueletterbible.org/lang/lexicon/lexicon.cfm?Strongs=H7626&t=KJV, accessed on May 30, 2018.
5. "Definition of Staff," *Blue Letter Bible*, https://www.blueletterbible.org/lang/lexicon/lexicon.cfm?Strongs=H4938&t=KJV, accessed on May 30, 2018.

6. "Definition of Etymology," *Merriam-Webster's Dictionary*, https://www.merriam-webster.com/dictionary/etymology, accessed on May 15, 2018.
7. "Definition of Comfort," *Merriam-Webster's Dictionary*, https://www.merriam-webster.com/dictionary/comfort, accessed on May 30, 2018.
8. Ibid.

WEEK 5

1. "Definition of Vex," *Merriam-Webster's Dictionary*, https://www.merriam-webster.com/thesaurus/vex, accessed on May 15, 2018.
2. Ibid, Keller, 138-140.
3. "Definition of Runneth Over," *Blue Letter Bible*, https://www.blueletterbible.org/lang/lexicon/lexicon.cfm?Strongs=H7310&t=KJV, accessed on May 30, 2018.
4. *The Original Aramaic New Testament in Plain English with Psalms & Proverbs, 8th Edition* (2007) via BibleHub.com.

WEEK 6

1. Corday, Ken and Nelson, Brent. "Theme from 'Days of Our Lives.'" Recorded February 2010. Track 1 on *Days of Our Lives Soundtrack*. La-La Land Records. Compact disc.

2. C. H. Spurgeon, *The Treasury of David, Volume 1* (New York: I.K. Funk & Company, 1882), 402.

3. Warren W. Wiersbe, *Be Worshipful* (Colorado Springs: David C. Cook, 2004), 95.

4. "The Compound Names of Jehovah," *Quizlet.com*, https://quizlet.com/193697150/the-compound-names-of-jehovah-flash-cards/, accessed on May 31, 2018.

5. Saul McLeod, "Maslow's Hierarchy of Needs," *SimplyPsychology*, May 21, 2018, https://www.simplypsychology.org/maslow.html.

6. Jalen Rose. Twitter Post. October 1, 2013, 5:24 a.m. https://twitter.com/jalenrose/status/385017465085755392?lang=en.